IT'S ALL ABOUT THE SALE

MASTERING THE PSYCHOLOGY OF SALES

IT'S ALL ABOUT THE SALE

MASTERING THE PSYCHOLOGY OF SALES

DR DEBRI VAN WYK

It's All About the Sale

All Rights Reserved 2020

© Debri van Wyk

No part of this may be reproduced, stored in a retrieval system, or transmitted by any means, electronic, mechanical, photocopying, recording, or otherwise, without permission from the author.

ISBN: 9798647094391

Imprint: Independently published

Copyright Material

Printed in the United States of America

Contents

About The Author 1

Introduction 2

The Psychology Of Sales 4

The Customers' Pre-Sale Mind 28

Subconscious Selling 37

Emotional Intelligent Selling (Eqs) 46

Selling And Buying Personalities 69

The Sales Equation 85

The Sales Process 103

Sales And Technology 117

The Digital Sales Executive 136

ABOUT THE AUTHOR

DR DEBRI VAN WYK

Dr. Debri Van Wyk is a seasoned Organizational Psychologist, Serial Entrepreneur, and Author who loves fusing business and psychology to help professionals master the art of sales. He holds a Ph.D. in Industrial Psychology and a bachelor's degree in Marketing. Debri has decades of multi-industry and international experience and had served in various capacities that includes Psychometric testing expert, Leadership Coach and Talent advisor. He relishes capitalizing on the marvels of psychology to understand consumer-behaviour and structure the company's products & services in accordance with the consumer's needs.

Debri has founded multiple businesses relating to the industry of Human Resource Management, his current company being Strategic Talent Technologies. He has an incredible eye for assessing talent and loves grooming professionals and helping them reach their ultimate potential. Serving as the ambassador of leadership development, Debri shares an incredible passion for nurturing the leaders of tomorrow.

Debri strives to leverage his expertise in sales psychology and consumer-behaviour to help sales professionals nail the process of sales. He greatly values people's needs and consumer's requirements and aims to capitalize on psychological parameters to help salespeople comprehend consumer's demands. Debri spends his leisure hours in the company of his family and friends, playing golf, and on the occasion, a preacher who loves helping others build a better connection with God and recognize the true power of faith & generosity.

INTRODUCTION

For a salesperson to close sales faster and get bigger deals, one must have an understanding of the psychology of sales. Customers buy for different reasons, not necessarily for yours. They think and act differently, even though most of the time we assume otherwise. However, what is true for all customers is knowing how to create rapport and generate attention. And this is where we introduce "It's All About the Sale, Mastering the Psychology of Sales."

We must agree that whenever we contact a customer or a prospect for that matter, we tend to interrupt their day, which causes their defenses to rise. Therefore, if you do what most salespeople do and talk about *your* needs, you can be sure that you will not win their attention. It is essential to understand and accept that the initial step you should take is to create an environment that decreases stress for the customer and engages their sense of curiosity.

It's All About the Sale is a compilation of the latest research and practical examples that create a better understanding of the functioning of the brain and what is required to win a customer's attention and increase the possibility of making the sale. Selling begins with the right conversation, a collaborative attitude, and the mindset to work from the customer's point of view as opposed to yours. The goal of this book is to help salespeople close sales faster, to generate bigger deals, eliminate price as a significant differentiator, and to win customers for life.

It's All About the Sale will equip business leaders, entrepreneurs, and salespeople with actionable ideas to help them reach their goals quickly and successfully. The book is ideal for leaders in business and executives at all levels including sales executives, existing and upcoming entrepreneurs, and professional service providers. Every reader of this book will leave with actionable ideas that are implementable immediately to assist them in reaching their goals.

CHAPTER 1

THE PSYCHOLOGY OF SALES

Introduction

Finding the perfect salesperson is impossible. The main reason why sales managers fail to find good salespeople is that they believe that all salespeople are exactly the same in behavior, characteristics, skills, and abilities. However, sales, in general, is so complex that a good salesperson in one industry might not necessarily be a good salesperson in another industry. Someone good at selling cars might not be that good at selling insurance policies. One of the most critical questions hiring managers want to know is whether a potential salesperson can sell. This question is valid, but only half correct. A better question to ask is whether this potential salesperson can sell *my* product. The product and market prescribe the salesperson's behavioral and cognitive attributes required to be successful in sales.

It is also interesting how sales, in general, has changed over the past decade in terms of psychological principles. Selling is not just about supply and demand anymore, where your customer has a need and the seller has a product to supply. It's also not only about how well the salesperson can present a product or negotiate a price, or whether the salesperson has an extroverted personality and can easily interact with others. To be successful in sales, the salesperson must understand and appreciate the product they want to sell. They should also have specialist knowledge on who the potential buyer will be and have the ability to attract them, create an interest and desire in the product, and tap into the mind of the buyer to create excitement. As a salesperson, you also have to convince a customer, using this specialist knowledge and skills, not just to buy a specific product, but to buy that particular product *from you*.

The Marketing Effect

Have you ever bought something you didn't need or even something you didn't want? This is the art of good marketing and selling. The market today allows buyers to buy almost any product, at a price that suits them, at a time convenient to them. The traditional marketing channels do not work anymore because buyers have more choice and have become accustomed to *smart* marketing tactics. Selling is not only about the product anymore. It's not about the ability to identify a need or provide a buyer with options. Selling today is about solutions. The seller with the best solution will make the sale and, to find the best solution, the salesperson must understand how to utilize a product to fulfill more than its obvious use. Likewise, the salesperson must also understand the buyer's ability to see the solution as intended by the salesperson.

Example: If you want to sell a car, the apparent use of this product is to get a person from point A to point B. The typical marketing approach will be to describe the product in terms of safety, comfort, luxury, price, or various guarantees. Although that adds value to the car, it does not provide a distinct solution that will set your product apart from your competitors' products. A potential solution for your customer may be to sell the journey which only your product can guarantee. A father who wants to buy a car for his son who is going to university wants a vehicle that is safe and reliable. The solution is not just a car that is safe and reliable because he can find this product at most brands and dealerships. The solution might instead be to sell a car that his son can sell when he gets his first job after graduation. This solution does not just promote a vehicle that has a good trade-in value, but subconsciously assures the father that the car will be safe and reliable.

Another marketing technique used by salespeople is selling a lifestyle and how important it is that only their product can guarantee this lifestyle. Although this approach is very successful and is still used today, the long-term effect of this approach remains questionable. When a customer buys into this lifestyle, and the product fails to produce the promise made, the risk is not only losing a potential returning customer to your business, but a customer lost to your brand. This emphasizes the importance of understanding your customer and providing them with a solution that doesn't just sell a product but is an attempt to retain this customer and get repeated business from them.

Successful salespeople often focus on the feelings of their customers instead of logic, mainly because sales happen on impulse, which is driven by emotions and feelings. If a potential customer has time to think about buying something and takes time to reason through the deal, the impulse to buy a product becomes less, and selling this product is less likely. The psychology of selling is to provide your customer with a solution that will speak to both their emotions and logic.

Example: A customer who is very interested in a fast car will listen intently to a salesperson who talks about horsepower and kilowatts because it speaks to his emotions and feelings. But by adding the car's ability to stop in a very short distance and the car's ability to warn the driver of oncoming traffic, the salesperson then also appeals to the logical side of the customer, thus providing the potential buyer with a valid reason to buy this car.

The gaining vs losing effect

Every buyer has two motivations in common; they either want to gain something or are concerned that they might lose something if they don't buy a particular product. Being able to identify the reason behind your customer's buying motivation will give a salesperson an advantage over others. Research shows that people are significantly more afraid of losing something than gaining something. It, therefore, explains why selling something to a customer who needs to buy something in fear of losing out is easier than selling to someone who only wants to buy a product to have more than others.

 The losing effect, also described as loss aversion, is twice as powerful as gaining something. Amos Tversky and Daniel Kahneman found that someone who manages not to lose $100 is more satisfied than someone who just won $100. Loss aversion also plays a significant role in negotiating prices. A potential buyer is more inclined to agree to a higher price if the risk of losing the product is very high. A buyer who wants to trade in his second-hand car for a new car will be less likely to negotiate a better deal on the new car if the price on his old vehicle meets his expectations. If a dealership gives the potential buyer a much lower price for his old car, the potential buyer will either find another dealership who can offer him more or try to negotiate a better deal on the new car. Research suggests that people will pay more for a product if they feel they are treated fairly, like offering them a reasonable price for their old car.

The concept of framing is used in many marketing campaigns and has to do with how a product's price is structured. Offering a product at a discounted price may draw your customers' attention, but, offering a product at a discounted rate for a limited time only will attract even more attention. A limited product type sells much better than a limited product discount. The fear of losing out on a product is much greater than the fear of losing out on a discounted price.

Let's say, for example, the potential buyer wants to buy a new car that is worth $50 000, and the dealership can offer a $2 000 discount. The buyer wants to trade in his old vehicle as a deposit, and the value of the old car is $20 000. The salesperson can structure the deal in two ways:

1. Offer a discount on the new car and sell it at $48 000, and offer the customer $20 000 for his old car, or
2. Offer the new car at $50 000 and offer to trade the customer's old car for 10% above the old car's value.

In both cases, the total amount the customer will have to pay for his new car will be $28 000. However, the customer will be more prone to take option two because he might not get another offer of 10% higher for his old car, so the fear of loss will be higher than gaining the $2 000 discount. The importance of this example is not in the total cost of the new car, but in increasing the probability to make a sale.

The Brand Effect

The value of a brand, also known as brand equity, plays a vital role in marketing and selling. Brand equity is when customers are willing to pay more for a particular product than for a generic product. Brand equity usually sells prestige and sophistication, exceptional quality, or stock limitations.

Brand equity directly affects sales because customers prefer products with an excellent reputation. For example, when Apple releases a new product, customers will stand in line for hours to get their hands on this new product, even though the price of this product is much higher than its nearest competitor. The primary reason for this is because Apple has significant brand equity. Apple's brand equity is so strong that it has become the focal research of many scientists, from marketing to neuroscientists. A research study in 2011 showed that in some people, Apple products are triggering the same areas in the brain as religious imagery in a person of faith. In another study in 2008, again using the Apple brand, researchers found that being exposed to the Apple logo can make you more creative.

> *"Research shows that consistent, positive interactions with a brand create positive psychological reinforcement when it's encountered the next time. On the other hand, negative experiences can do just the opposite. Brands who deliver consistent, high-quality experiences across different touchpoints like retail, social, and customer service don't just win hearts — they actually win minds and change how we think."*
>
> **— Chris Bolman**

Brand equity impacts not only sales but also customer loyalty and retention. Selling a product from a reputable brand is probably easier than selling a generic product, especially if that brand comes with a significant customer loyalty base. The challenge, however, is not just in retaining them, but growing your brand. In an economy where price sometimes trumps quality, it creates new dynamics for the salesperson to sell a product that is significantly more expensive than its closest rival. Similarly, in a world where technology advances by the second, and where the difference in product specifications becomes less, the function of marketing and sales becomes more complex and challenging. Using Apple again as an example, the difference between the Apple iPhone and the Samsung Galaxy is minimal, with some saying the Galaxy might even be more advanced than the iPhone. However, the iPhone costs significantly more than the Samsung, so how does Apple keep its customers? On the contrary, how can Samsung convert more Apple customers to Samsung customers? This is the complexity of the Brand Effect on sales.

From a sales perspective, we must focus on selling a product with strong brand equity against the selling of a generic product.

Brand equity	Generic brand
<ul><li>Quality over price</li><li>Price insensitive</li><li>Limited product range</li><li>Status</li><li>Market specific</li><li>Brand conscious</li></ul>	<ul><li>Price over quality</li><li>Affordable</li><li>Availability of products</li><li>Usability</li><li>Open market</li></ul>

Products with a strong brand equity

Selling products with strong brand equity will usually focus more on the quality of the product than the price. Customers who buy these products will place a higher value on products that have a limited product range, which will make the customer unique in owning this product. They are very status-driven and enjoy the recognition that this product brings. The market usually has particular demographics with customers who are brand conscious.

Products with a generic brand

Products that do not have strong brand equity attract customers who consider price over quality. They look for products that are affordable and readily available. Customers who buy these products are more concerned with the usability of the product. The market is large and has diverse demographics with customers who are less concerned with the brand and more concerned about affordability.

The Social Effect[1]

Human beings are social creatures by nature. We always compare ourselves with others before buying something. The effect of social media and big brands sponsoring well-known people to market their products is with the use of the social effect to create more customers. The challenge for marketing departments is how they advertise their product so that more people can associate with the brand and compare themselves to others who will buy this product.

Salespeople can use the social effect to their advantage when trying to sell their products. Still, they should also be careful in associating too much with a person like a professional athlete, a music icon, or a popular actor. The marketing value such people bring to a product can be immense; however, when this person does something that does not align with the products they sponsor, it may harm the brand and product. There are numerous examples of celebrities who damaged the brands that sponsored them, with some losing that sponsorship. David Warner lost his sponsorship with Asics after the ball-tampering scandal

---

[1] This section only provides an overview of how social media affects sales. The use of social media in selling is discussed in chapter 8

against the South African cricket team. Accenture dropped Tiger Woods after his sex scandal, and Maria Sharapova lost her Tag Heuer sponsorship after her doping ban. Oscar Pistorius lost his sponsorships from Nike and Oakley after murdering his girlfriend. Nike also ended its sponsorship with Lance Armstrong because of his doping scandal.

Even though we know about these scandals and how they can damage a brand's reputation, the benefits of using the social effect in sales still outweigh the risks as discussed above. It is, however, essential to remember that the social effect can be both positive and negative for your product, so always ensure you have an exit strategy when signing deals with celebrities before they tarnish your brand.

Another significant impact of the social effect is the role of social media in selling. The fact that more people use the internet to learn more about a specific product or to even buy that product directly from the internet has placed the typical salesperson without the so-called *walk-in* customer. The approach we must take in the future is not to wait for the *walk-in* customer, but to become the *walk-to* salesperson. We have to meet the customers where they do their buying, which is on social media.

Customers are evolving from walk-in to log-in.

Research is showing us that 91% of business to business (B2B) buyers are active and involved in social media, 84% of senior executives use social media to support buying decisions, 84% of teenagers use Facebook and 37% use Instagram. If our market spends most of its time on these social networks, then this is where we should sell our products.

The internet is about connecting people, and social media is about building relationships. Thus, selling to customers cannot be done without being connected to the online community.

Psychological attributes of the salesperson

In the previous section, we mentioned that salespeople are not all the same when it comes to behavior and characteristics. In a recent study conducted in one of the more prominent motor brands in South Africa, salespeople were asked to rate themselves on a list of 50 behavioral attributes on a 5-point scale, five being "Describes me completely" and 1 "Does not describe me at all". Out of 50 behavioral attributes, only six were similar in the group of salespeople. Although behavioral attributes are essential, it is important first to understand the product and market they are required to sell.

For any salesperson to be successful, they have to possess certain qualities and characteristics. They have to continually develop these skills to enable themselves to become better salespeople.

Quality 1: Assertiveness

To be assertive means being able to stand up for your own or other people's rights calmly and positively, without being either aggressive or passively accepting 'wrong'. Assertive people know what they want and aren't afraid to ask for it. They also respect the feelings and needs of others and are prepared to negotiate solutions that are acceptable to both sides.

Salespeople may, at times, be too forceful or aggressive, and other times too passive. Aggressive people want to win at all costs and may push a customer away from a sale. Passive people, on the other hand, will give in too quickly and will be prepared to lose out on a deal to keep the other party happy.

Some people also make the mistake of thinking assertiveness is all about the tone of your voice. However, assertiveness is much more than just the sound of your voice but plays a significant role in body posture. The research suggested that 55%

of the message you convey when you meet people is through your body language, so to ensure you initiate a sale even before you begin selling, start with assertiveness.

To be more assertive, you can practice the following:

a. Value yourself, your skills, and your abilities: If you doubt your talents and skills, others will pick up on it, and they will also question your ability. Trust in your ability to sell.
b. Speak up: Speaking softly might create the perception that you are unsure of yourself or the product you are trying to sell. In speaking up, your customer will hear you clearly and also find you more convincing.
c. Express yourself positively: When you are positive, your customers become positive. Don't talk about how expensive your product is in comparison to other products, but instead sell it as quality worth paying.
d. Learn to say NO: A *yes man* or *people pleaser* might make the sale initially but will realize that negotiating will be less effective; making the best deal will favor only the customer, and their own sales margins will diminish.
e. Listen: Customers might perceive a salesperson who does not listen as aggressive or non-interested in the customers' needs. Listening and responding to your customers will ensure that you can offer your customer what they need or want, but also that you can negotiate better to make the deal beneficial for both you and the customer.
f. Communicate directly: When you express yourself directly and non-defensively, you give yourself the best chance to have a meaningful conversation. It also provides a more specific discussion that relates to the product you are trying to sell and not wasting time trying to convince a customer that you can sell something, but never actually getting to the sale.

g. Use "I" statements: Using statements like: I can offer you ... or I can arrange ... or I have this product available ... will convince the customer that you are taking ownership of this deal and that you will be responsible for ensuring you meet the customer's needs.
h. Keep emotions intact: A person who cannot manage their emotions may come across as erratic and impulsive. It is vital to show powerful emotions like optimism, empathy, and self-confidence, but not emotions that are aggressive, passive, or negative.
i. Appearance says everything: Dress to impress. A person who is underdressed or overdressed may create the wrong impression with the customer. If you sell a high-end vehicle for businesspeople, denim and sneakers might make the customer perceive the product as low quality. If you sell off-road vehicles in a 5-piece suit, your customer might also view the car as an oversized city driving vehicle.
j. Always be respectful: A good salesperson must respect the customer as much as the process. The customer might not always know what they want or need, and it's the responsibility of the salesperson to respect the customer enough to guide them in the right direction for the customer, and not just about making a sale. The sales process must be respected at all times. To rush the process or skip essential steps will negatively impact your sales.
k. Keep perspective: Bringing perspective to the sales process, salespeople equip their customers to find what they want and need, because they can see the customer's challenges in new and different ways. Usually, customers know what they want, but when a salesperson provides another perspective as to why the customer might wish

to buy this product, they will increase the probability to make the sale.
l. Know your product: One of the most important attributes of an assertive salesperson is their ability to give expert advice and input on the product they are selling. When a customer asks a question about your product that is not so obvious or "visible on the package", a good salesperson who knows the product very well will be able to answer confidently without making things up.

Quality 2: Confidence

Confident people tend to be more successful in all areas of life, especially in sales. Customers tend to trust salespeople if they are confident and knowledgeable about their product or service and can sell it with great self-belief. Selling a product or service is more than just selling or knowing about the product or service but having the confidence in your ability to influence people to buy your product.

When your customer has doubts or worries about the product you are selling, they might doubt the product, but most times their concerns stem from your ability to convince them that this product is what they need and want. This ability to convince people is why having confidence in yourself and your product is so important. Sales are all about accomplishing a transfer of trust. If you can transfer your faith in the product over to your customer so that they have confidence in your product, then the sale is made.

Our brains desire conformity, agreement, and congruency. What we perceive or take in through our senses must match what the reality in our head understands. If our perceptions do not match the reality in our head, then our brain will modify the story to make it match, even if it has to change what you perceived or took in through your senses.

There's a popular demonstration of this that's been done in a psychology class. A man jumps up in class and stabs another man with a banana. The other man—who's in on it—has a fake blood package strapped to his body, stumbles to the ground, causing a big red mess. The other man escapes. Police come to the scene and interview the students who witnessed this. When questioned, the students describe a knife in great detail—even though what they saw was a banana. Their brains knew that you couldn't stab someone with a banana, so they just assumed it was a knife. They made the perception match the story.

As a salesperson, your sales pitch must match the expectations of the customer, without trying to convince them that your product is superior to your competitor's product.

"The power in the delivery of a message will always be stronger than the message itself."

The only way to make the delivery of the message more powerful is to deliver it with confidence.

To be more confident, you can practice the following:

a. Become an expert at the basics: Before you can sell anything, make sure you understand the sales process. Know the different stages in selling and understand each step and what you and the customer requires. If you can't do the basics well, you will never master the complexity of sales.

b. Know your product (again): As you've already learned in the previous section on assertiveness, knowing your product will also make you more confident in selling the product. If you can answer your customer on any questions they might have regarding the product, it will make you feel more confident, and you will also transfer confidence to your customer.

c. Build on your strengths: Confident salespeople know their strengths, and they build on these strengths to become better at selling. It is essential to differentiate between confidence and arrogance. Arrogance cannot replace confidence and will always alienate your customers instead of building a relationship.
d. Surround yourself with positivity and success: The more you are around people who are positive and successful, the more you will become positive and learn to be successful. Positive and optimistic people motivate others to be successful, so even if you don't have someone on your team who is positive and optimistic, find a mentor who can help you become more positive and build on your success.
e. Never settle for mediocrity: Confident salespeople always want to achieve and be the best at what they are doing. If you resolve to be mediocre, then your confidence will be mediocre. Strive to be the best, and your confidence will follow.
f. Take an emotional dipstick: Before approaching a customer, check your state of emotional wellbeing. If you don't feel optimistic or you feel down, be careful when approaching your customer, because they will sense your emotional wellbeing and might perceive it as low confidence. This is also true for yourself; not feeling optimistic will also negatively impact your confidence and selling ability.

Quality 3: Ambition

A salesperson without ambition is simply a person trying to make a living by selling a product. Salespeople must have a strong ambition to succeed and a drive to be the best at what they are doing. Salespeople with strong ambition regularly analyze their achievements versus aspirations to ensure they are continually growing and achieving success.

It is vitally important for salespeople to clarify their ambition, be clear about what they want to achieve, what it looks like for them, by when they want to achieve it, and how will they know that they've achieved it. Without a clear understanding of what they want to achieve, their ambition becomes less forceful, their drive to achieve drops, and they become more passive in attaining their ambitions.

Your ambition must also align with realistic outcomes and reachable targets. Achieving your goals is important for sustainable motivation and drive.

> *"Ambition is the fuel for motivation."*

To be more ambitious, you can practice the following:

a. Take risks: If you want to achieve, you have to take risks. Ambitious people are not afraid of taking a leap of faith and experimenting with ideas. Some people are risk-averse and may tend to follow the tried and tested methods. For salespeople, however, tried and tested techniques may not always bring the best results. Taking risks can lead to taking a loss, but when you get it right, the reward can be so much more significant.

b. Don't wait for the doors to open: In an aggressive sales environment, one cannot wait for the perfect moment. An ambitious salesperson will take a moment and make it perfect. Don't wait for opportunities to come your way; be actively on the lookout for opportunities.

Waiting for opportunities is wasting opportunities.

c. Set SMART goals: Setting goals for yourself to achieve, be it daily, weekly or monthly goals is important to keep motivating yourself to succeed. Make sure your goals are SMART; this means your goals are:

   I. **S**pecific: Well defined, clear, and unambiguous
  II. **M**easurable: With specific criteria that measure your progress
 III. **A**chievable: Attainable and not impossible to achieve
  IV. **R**ealistic: Within reach, practical, and relevant
   V. **T**imely: With a clearly defined timeline, starting dates, and target dates.

d. Focus on gains and not losses: Focusing on what you might lose will negatively influence your ambition, but focusing on what you might gain will motivate you to work harder and drive you to achieve great results. What you focus on will eventually become your reality.

e. Failure is the beginning of success: "Anyone who has never made a mistake has never tried anything new" - Albert Einstein. You cannot succeed at something if you haven't learned to fail at it. Luck is if you're successful at something without trying and failing a couple of times. Ambitious people will do whatever it takes to win, even if it means failing 100 times.

Most people have attained their greatest success just one step beyond their greatest failure. - **Napoleon Hill**

f. Get going on execution: You can't execute something if you don't start. There's no point in starting something if you don't plan to complete it. Ambitious people focus as much on starting with something as they are on executing and finishing it. Ambition is not just about having a good idea and "seeing" the possible results but is working towards and achieving those results.

g. Use your imagination: Ambitious people always look for different ways to achieve their goals. They don't allow traditions and norms to hold them back from achievement and will apply creative problem solving to achieve their goals.
h. It is doable: Never let anyone tell you that something is impossible to do or to achieve. Having a "can do" attitude separates successful people from the average. Ambitious people are always open-minded and flexible in how they see problems and opportunities.

Quality 4: Enthusiasm

Enthusiastic people work harder and find enjoyment in what they do. One of the most important questions any person should ask themselves is what makes them passionate, what are they motivated by, what do they enjoy doing and what do they see themselves doing for the next 10 – 15 years. Selling can be one of the most engaging careers one can have, but it can also be one of the most draining jobs. Although selling skills can be learned, selling behavior and a preference for selling is rooted deep in one's personality.

Another critical factor is how much you believe in the product or service you are trying to sell. If you don't believe in the product, you will be less enthusiastic when selling it. If you are not interested in cars, then selling them will be a challenge because your enthusiasm will be low. The same is also true about passion for a specific brand. If you believe in a particular brand, it will be easy to sell the brand because you will be enthusiastic about it. For example, if you believe the Apple iPhone is superior to any other phone in the market and you are only interested in ever owning an Apple iPhone, then selling a Samsung or Nokia phone might be more challenging.

Enthusiasm as an emotion is projected in your non-verbal behavior, facial expressions, and tone of voice. Someone enthusiastic about a product will be more positive and friendly, which will be evident in the sound of their voice, more positive facial expressions, and even how they walk or sit will be more energetic.

To be more enthusiastic, you can practice the following:

a. Find a deeper connection with the product or brand you are selling: When you identify better with the product, you will be more enthusiastic about it, and customers will find it easier to relate to what you are trying to sell. When your customers start sharing your enthusiasm for the product, selling it will then be much easier.

b. Be curious: The first question you should ask yourself is why you like the product you are trying to sell? What about this product makes you excited? Why would you like to own this product (if you don't own it already)? Now ask the question, why would my customers want to own this product? What about this product makes my customers excited? Be curious, ask questions, and share why this product is so excellent.

c. Know the company: Every product or brand belongs to a company. To believe in a product is to believe in the company. Learn more about the company: what are their values, core beliefs, history, and future goals. How can you relate to the company? Why do you want to work at this company? Being able to identify with the company and its values will make you more enthusiastic about working for the company and about being an ambassador for their products.

d. What is your purpose? Many salespeople do not understand what their purpose is. If your goal is to sell products, then your enthusiasm will eventually fade away. You have to find a purpose and meaning behind what you do.

Your purpose might be much bigger than the purpose of the product you are selling, or you might believe in the positive impact the product can make, that your purpose is in selling the positive impact and not a product per se. Your purpose for selling should be bigger than just paying the bills.

Quality 5: Resourcefulness

Resourcefulness is about finding a way to achieve something. Resourcefulness inspires an out-of-the-box thinking mindset, coming up with new ideas, becoming more inventive and creative in selling something. Resourcefulness is especially important in difficult times, in trying to sell a complex product or in selling to a demanding customer. A good salesperson will be resourceful to sell a product to someone when the average salesperson fails to do so. Salespeople who are not resourceful will accept failure more quickly and give up before trying all the different potential solutions.

Being resourceful is not just about being creative but also knowing what resources are available to secure a sale. Resources can be other people who can help you convince a demanding customer, having brochures close by to support what you say about a product, and value-added products to make your product more attractive to the customer. It's about being able to restructure a deal to make it more appealing to your customer, and it's about learning more about your competitor's product to sell your product better.

To be more resourceful, you can practice the following:

a. Always believe in alternatives: It is crucial that you always believe in an alternative way of solving a problem. Finding alternatives will force you to always be on the lookout for other resources to solve a problem.

b. Concentrate on the outcome, not the process: If you focus on the process, your thoughts and actions will define the requirements in that moment or stage of the process. You will not see the end goal and other potential ways of achieving the outcome. If you focus on the outcome, you will be more open to considering other resources to solve a problem.
c. Be persistent: Having a "never give up" attitude will open up a world of opportunities to achieve your goals. By being persistent, you will look for resources in more ways, because the focus is not just on succeeding in step 1, but to push through to the end.
d. If others can't do it, then I'll be the first: Most people give up the moment they learn that all other people failed at it already. They give up quickly because they believe that everyone else already tried everything, so why should they try? Having an attitude of solving a problem at all costs, regardless of whether it's been resolved before or not, will force you to look at other resources that others never considered.
e. It can be more than one resource: Sometimes solving a problem or selling a product might require you to find more than one resource to succeed. Many salespeople will try one or two different resources but not succeed. The problem might not have been the resources they tried, but the fact that they tried them independently of each other. Good salespeople can pull different resources together to achieve a goal.
f. Read, read, and read: The more you read about the product you are selling, the more you will learn about the product and become more resourceful in finding a way to sell it. Read about other products that are associated with your product, read about your competitors' products. The more you know, the better you can sell.

Quality 6: Initiative

Taking the initiative means being proactive and doing something without waiting for instructions. In a sales environment, being proactive is critical to generating leads, customers, and sales. Salespeople who are more reactive and waiting for a potential customer to come to them might find their selling pipeline empty most of the time. They will also find it difficult to project future sales or know how to approach customers differently. By taking the initiative, good salespeople can proactively look for new customers, be ready to provide the customer with a solution and sell a product to a customer even before they need it.

One of the biggest challenges facing salespeople today is their lack of taking the initiative and waiting for instructions from their managers. Because they focus more on the walk-in or phone-in customer, they are less prepared to offer a solution to help the customer, and the customer might feel that this company does not understand their key concerns and needs.

To take better initiative, you can practice the following:

a. Identify your key customers or prospects: When you identify your key customers or prospective customers, you can better prepare to support them. You will also know where to find them, the best way to market to them, and the best approach to gain their trust.
b. Study your market: In knowing your market, economic trends, and technological advancements, you can take the initiative to support them without them having to approach you. It will show your interest in their specific business that you took the initiative to understand their daily challenges.
c. Detect and correct: Keep a close eye on your sales margins, targets, and projections. If you detect that you might not achieve your goals, implement correction steps as soon

as possible. If you are proactive in managing your targets and projections, you will have more time available to find alternative ways or solutions to minimize the loss of not making your target. If you leave it to the end, you won't have the time or resources available to find alternative ways of minimizing the loss.

Miss your market, miss your target

d. Always know more than your customer: Today's world, where information is available at the click of a button, and where technology enables your customers to learn everything about your products and more, places a lot of pressure on salespeople to be experts in their fields. This is why salespeople must be proactive and continually learn more about their products, as well as supporting products and their competitors' products.

e. Get real-time feedback: Most salespeople never ask for feedback when they lose a deal or if the sale doesn't realize. They try to cope with the disappointment or rejection from the customer instead of asking for feedback. This feedback is more than just about the product and price, but about your interaction with them, the quality of service you provided your behavior and selling style. Getting real-time feedback will help you grow and ensure whatever you might've done wrong with the previous customer will not happen again in the future.

Conclusion

The psychology of sales is the understanding of behavior and everything that affects behavior and decisions. It is crucial to understand that buying behavior impacts a myriad of things, including emotions, brands, and marketing techniques. Companies invest large sums of money in analyzing their customers and the market, however spending little on those who must find the customers and sell the products. The more salespeople understand what influences their customers to buy, the better they will be at selling. We've discussed the marketing effect and how customers are more inclined to buy because of their fear of losing out, but it's merely scratching the surface in terms of the customer's mind and behavior. We have to ensure, though, that we have the best salespeople in place, continually develop them, and provide appropriate reward structures.

CHAPTER 2

THE CUSTOMERS' PRE-SALE MIND

Introduction

Potential customers want to know four things before they buy from you. However, they never ask these questions, and as the salesperson, you can't directly answer them either. The only way to answer these questions is to influence and convince your customer through your selling behavior and intentions. In this section, we look at how you, as a salesperson, can connect with and influence your customers.

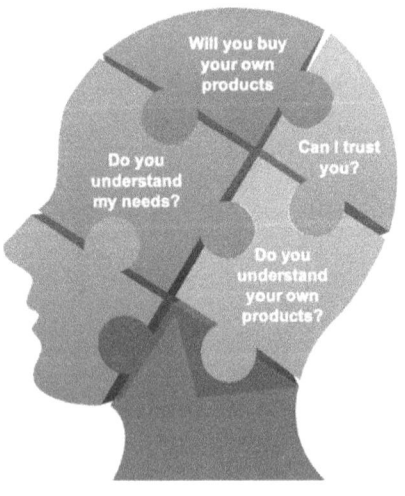

Can I trust you?

The first question customers ask before buying something is whether they can trust you. Unfortunately, due to the nature of sales and how it's rewarded, like high commission structures, some salespeople will try numerous techniques to make a sale. We all know the reputation some second-hand salespeople have in the industry to sell cars without giving the customer all the necessary information to make an informed decision, or sometimes bloating the price of the vehicle.

Steve W. Martin conducted a research study on salespeople. He found that customers rate two-thirds of salespeople as being average or poor, and only 18% of salespeople are classified as trusted advisors whom they respect.

> *"I'm not upset that you lied to me, I'm upset that from now on I can't believe you."*
>
> **— Friedrich Nietzsche**

When customers trust you as a salesperson, they believe in your promises and will listen to your advice.

Over 90% of companies indicated that they only do business with other companies or salespeople they can trust. Like the second-hand car salesperson, there is a general distrust in salespeople. Sometimes salespeople come across as pushy and trying to make a sale regardless of the customer's needs. Customers cited five reasons why they sometimes find it challenging to work with a salesperson:

1. The salesperson tried too hard to make the sale
2. They couldn't communicate effectively
3. Their personality style was too different
4. The age difference was too much
5. The salesperson was too eager to make friends

There is a point where the customer respects the salesperson's advice and is not offended by their influence, and that builds the relationship. Once you build trust with your customers, they are more likely to return to you in the future and will also recommend you to other potential customers. Customers who receive excellent service from a reliable salesperson will usually tell other people about the product but emphasize the service they received from that specific salesperson.

Building trust starts with you, the salesperson. Customers will sense whether they can trust you within the first 30 seconds of meeting you, and it will be up to you to validate that they can trust you, or convince them to trust you through your behavior and response to questions. Certain behaviors can build trust when applied with pure intentions.

An article titled "Four Behaviors to Building Trust in Sales" by David Jacoby, indicated that salespeople could build trust through four behaviors:

1. Reliability

Reliability is about keeping your promises and never overpromising. Manage your customers' expectations and do not surprise them with information that could've influenced their decision to buy.

2. Honesty

A salesperson never (or mostly never) intends to lie to get a sale. Still, they quickly fall into the trap of bending the information and omitting or misrepresenting information that can influence the customer's decisions. You must always answer all your customer's questions honestly, even if you have to tell the customer that you are not sure but will get back to them as soon as possible. Honesty also includes being transparent in your product and whether your product can fulfill the customer's need. Bad-mouthing a competitor is an indication of low self-confidence and an intention to be dishonest.

3. Responsiveness

You must respond to your customers as soon as possible. A customer who feels that the salesperson is wasting time or not getting back to them at an agreed time will think that they cannot trust this salesperson. Your customer needs to know that they are a priority and that you will try your best to fulfill their requirements. Some people are of the perception that if they don't have new information to share, then there is no point in contacting the customer. This, unfortunately, is not what the customer expects or thinks when they don't get any feedback from the salesperson. As a salesperson, you should be responsive and give feedback, even if there is no new information. The customer will feel that they are still a priority.

4. Objectivity

To be objective is sometimes very difficult, especially in a sales environment. Your responsibility as a salesperson is to convince the customer that your product is the ideal solution to their needs. But what if your product is not ideal and you know of a product that will fulfill their needs better? Objectivity is one of the most powerful trust-builders because your customers will notice that your interest is in supporting them, and they will see you as a trustworthy advisor and will always come back to you for advice. Just maybe *your* product will be the ideal product for the customer in the future.

Salespeople who cannot be trusted are missing out on a powerful differentiator.

Do you understand my needs?

The only way to give your customers excellent service is to understand their needs. You can have the best product in the world, but if it doesn't fulfill the client's needs, then the product is of no value to them. You should know your customers' needs well enough to anticipate or sometimes predict what they expect from you.

To understand your customers' needs, you have to make a concerted effort to gather as much information about the customer as possible. A fundamental question most salespeople neglect to inquire about is, "why is the customer interested in your product?". Salespeople spend a lot of time and effort understanding what product the customer wants or needs, and whether they can fulfill this need. However, when the salesperson starts asking the customer why they need the product, they get a different perspective that they can use to influence a customer to buy from them. It is, however, critical to ask this question in an inquiring way and not a skeptical way or questioning the customer's need for this product. Example: A customer wants to buy a car that is fuel-efficient and reliable. If you ask the customer *what* car he wants to buy, he may answer a vehicle that is fuel-efficient and reliable. However, if you change the question from *what* to *why* he wants to buy the car, he might give you more information that will enable you to identify a more suitable vehicle and increase the probability of a sale.

Customers' needs can be grouped into four categories, and these categories can help you better understand their needs and influence them to buy your product. Figure 2.1 illustrates the FRAP method that can be used to help you better understand your customers' needs.

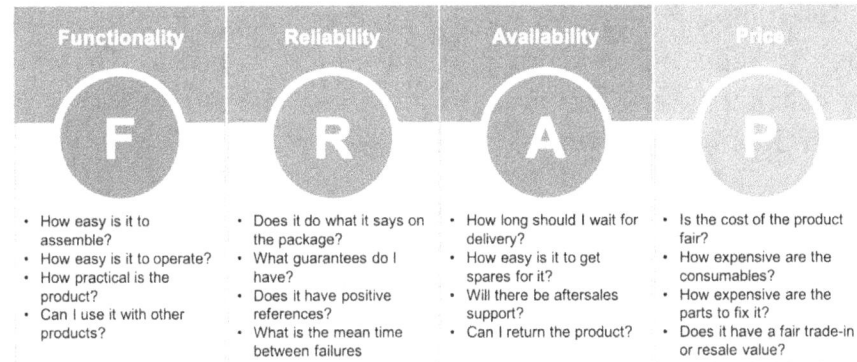

Figure 2.1 The FRAP method explaining customers' needs.

Do you know and understand your products?

Customers consistently gauge whether you have the product knowledge for the product you are trying to sell. Product knowledge shows the customer that they can trust you and the product. When you understand the features of your product, it will enable you to persuade the customer positively and enthusiastically. Your in-depth knowledge will show your customers that *you* trust and value your product, making it easier for them to trust your product as well. Customers respond better to salespeople who are enthusiastic and passionate about their products.

Knowledge is power

There is, however, more to product knowledge than *knowledge* alone. Understanding your product is equally important, if not more important in the sales process. The difference between product knowledge and product understanding is that *knowledge* is the facts and figures. In contrast, *understanding* is the ability to interpret those facts and figures and how they affect the customer. Having product *knowledge* and *understanding* will help you sell other features and benefits to the customer and influence their sales decision.

The FRAP method can also be used to test your product knowledge and understanding of what you are selling, as depicted in Figure 2.2.

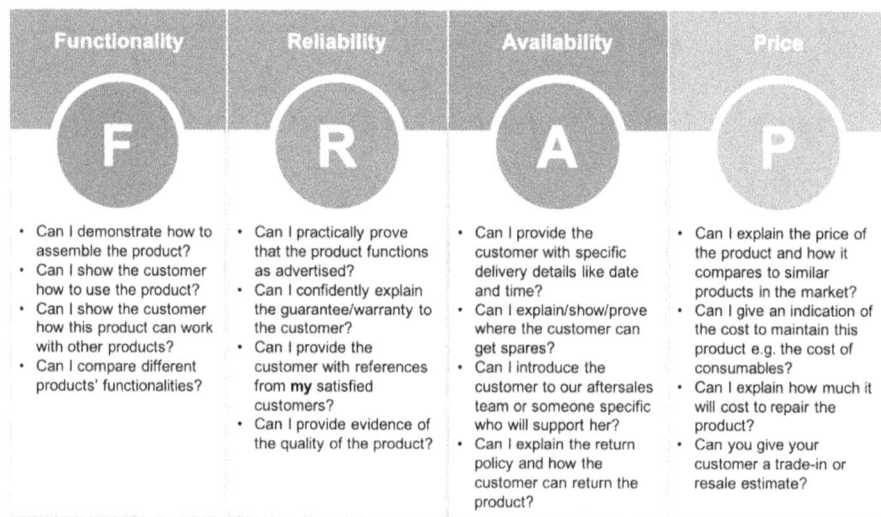

Figure 2.2 The FRAP method explaining the salespersons' product knowledge and understanding.

It is relatively easy to learn more about the product and gain the necessary knowledge, but as explained before, the understanding part is crucial. To enable you to understand the product better, you have to use the product yourself or have practical and hands-on experience. As you gain more knowledge and understanding of your product, ask yourself the questions as depicted in Figure 2.1 and 2.2 and ensure you can confidently answer all the questions.

Will you buy your products?

Are you your customer? Nothing says you trust and believe in your product as much as your willingness to buy and use your product. It does happen that salespeople sell products that they can't use or afford, but in general, if you can prove to your customer that you trust the product because you use it yourself, you will get better buy-in.

The best way to sell a product is to be an advertisement.

To be honest and transparent with your customers, you have to believe in your product so much that you won't buy any other product. If you want to promote your product as the best in its class, then you should personally use it as well.

When you buy your products, you get first-hand experience with the customer service you received and the value your company places on the products you are trying to sell. You can quickly identify any faults in your marketing strategy, sales process, customer service, aftersales service, product quality, and price. In identifying these faults early in the process, you can ensure that your customers don't experience similar issues when they buy from you. You can also better advise your customers on this process because you have first-hand experience going through the sales process.

Buying your products also makes you a brand ambassador for your company. Large companies invest large sums of money to get famous people to be their brand ambassadors. If you think of Nespresso, you think of George Clooney, and if you think Nike, you think of Tiger Woods. People trust a product more quickly when they see other people endorse it, especially famous people. It gives them a sense of comfort that if other people are using it, then it should be a good product. Your role as a salesperson is *as* important as your role as a brand ambassador.

Using your products shows that you trust your product. When you build trust with your customer, they will also trust your product, because they trust you. The best way to sell your product is to be a walking and talking advertisement for your product.

Conclusion

Sales success depends mostly on the trust relationship a customer has with the salesperson and the product. This trust relationship can be established even before the salesperson attempts a sales pitch, and the salesperson must be confident in their product, its usability, and how it will benefit the customer. The FRAP method is easy to learn and understand, but at the same time critical to apply. Your ability to communicate the functionality, reliability, availability, and price will impact the probability of the sale.

CHAPTER 3

SUBCONSCIOUS SELLING

Introduction

Science has captured the world of sales and that cannot be ignored or underestimated. The science of the mind has allowed major brands to read what we think and subconsciously influence our buying behavior. Through science, these brands can influence us to buy their product instead of a competitors' product at a lower price.

To understand subconscious selling and how it impacts our world today, we have to take a step back in history. Subliminal selling, or "mass manipulation" (later referred to as mass persuasion) can be found as far back as the early 1900s. Edward Bernays, an Austrian-American pioneer in the field of public relations and propaganda, and coincidently, also related to Sigmund Freud, used Freud's ideas to convince the public to believe in a particular theory or buy a specific brand of products. However, his work with "hidden messages" to influence buying behavior was considered unethical or even described as the "dark side of advertising", but it still serves as the beginning of subconscious selling as we know it today.

> *"The conscious and intelligent manipulation of the organized habits and opinions of the masses is an important element in democratic society. Those who manipulate this unseen mechanism of society constitute an invisible government which is the true ruling power of our country. We are governed, our minds are molded, our tastes formed, and our ideas suggested, largely by men we have never heard of.... It is they who pull the wires that control the public mind"*
>
> **— Edward Bernays**

There is a thin line between persuading and manipulating. Neuroscientists and marketers call this persuading, where critics call it manipulation. Whichever way we look at it, it is practiced by thousands of companies around the world, all fighting for your attention, whether consciously or subconsciously.

Furthermore, technology has taken subconscious selling to a level that is difficult to describe. Where static ads and one-liner marketing slogans attempt to subconsciously influence customers, technology has enabled this art to influence people in a millisecond or even microsecond where the customers don't even realize they were influenced to notice a specific product. Unlike the Matrix, where Neo had a choice between the red and blue pill, customers today have to take in this marketing attack of subconscious advertisements and somehow sift through all the information to make an informed decision. The question is, however, how informed are we, or are we influenced in such a way that shapes our belief that *we* are making an informed decision, an *informed decision* proudly sponsored by the brand you are about to buy?

How do they get this information?

Before we delve deeper into learning about different subconscious selling techniques used today, it is vital to understand how they obtain this information.

First, you are not as unique as you think you are. People share specific attributes, interests, values, personality styles, likes, and dislikes. Neuroscience taps into these characteristics and, using large samples of data, they can predict with a high level of accuracy, what you might want or need. Research shows that people with a specific personality style might be more prone to buy a particular type of car or wear certain types of clothes. So, if I know your personality, I can influence you to buy a particular kind of car. It is more complicated than this but based on the same principles.

The sophisticated approach to gathering data involves the Electroencephalogram or EEG. The EEG measures brain waves through frequencies so that every thought we think and emotion we feel can be detected. These frequencies can be detected whether we are aware of what we think or feel, or whether it is happening subconsciously.

Another method of measuring how the brain works is through functional magnetic resonance imaging or fMRI. The fMRI can pick up any changes in your brain that activates in different situations. It provides information on people's reasoning style, how they make decisions, form memories, and experience emotions.

Eye-tracking is also one of the ways neuro marketers can observe where we look first, what draws our attention, and where we start processing information when we walk into a grocery store. It also tells us how much time we spend looking at a specific product.

Physical excitement or arousal increases your heart rate, and neuro marketers use this technique to measure the impact of their product on your heart rate. Depending on the product they want to sell, they will want an increase or decrease in heart rate.

Subconscious Selling Techniques

"The business man's hunt for sales boosters is leading him into a strange wilderness; the subconscious mind."

—Wall Street Journal

Subconscious selling, or subliminal messaging, is a message formed to bypass our ordinary perceptions and observations. In some radio and television ads, this is a sound which is inaudible to the conscious mind but audible to the subconscious mind, or an image that is transmitting in milliseconds and unperceived consciously yet perceived subconsciously.

The importance of subconscious selling and how it can be used in everyday selling should never be to manipulate but to influence a customer to buy our products positively. From the examples below, you will recognize the subtle influences that are used by marketing and sales gurus to affect you. But, in understanding these techniques, you can also apply them to your selling techniques.

Experience

Most customers want to shop at malls that have plenty to offer, an environment that provides emotional, visual, and auditory entertainment, and now more than ever; it must be a shopping experience. It's not just about doing shopping but going shopping.

The solution is not just about the price but instead offering a variety of products or options. The environment must allow your customers to be confident when buying from you; they must feel relaxed but also excited about the buy and feel welcomed.

It is normal for car salespeople to take their customers on a test drive, which is a form of creating an experience. However, a customer expects this service, so it doesn't generate that level of excitement the customer subconsciously wants. The challenge for car salespeople is to create an experience that will influence a customer in such a way, that they would rather buy a car from you instead of your competitor (which could be your colleague next to you trying to sell to the same customer).

Employee training

Employees who are trained on company values, product specifications, and what words to use or not use when talking with customers, stand a much better chance of subconsciously influencing a customer to buy.

Salespeople who can empathize with a customer, making them feel good from the moment they walk into the shop, and giving them the brand experience the customer is used to, will find it easier to sell a product. Employees at Apple are trained a certain way, and regardless of the Apple store you visit worldwide, the shopping experience will always be the same because of the consistent employee training.

Body language

A happy customer is a returning customer. A salesperson can change a customers' day into a good or bad day by their non-verbal behavior. A salesperson who doesn't smile when they greet a customer can lose a sale even before a word is said. At the same time, a confident salesperson, who looks the customer in the eyes when talking to them, is dressed appropriately, and has open body language, will be closer to a sale before saying anything.

93% of our communication is non-verbal, with 55% being body language and 38% tone of voice. Influencing your customer to buy from you can be as easy as a simple smile.

Lighting

Light creates a visual effect in terms of image, shape, intensity, perception, and contrast; it has biological and psychological effects that impact the health and wellbeing of humans.

Depending on your product and brand, lights may be used to influence a customer to buy from you. Lights set the mood for the customer, and if the feeling matches the experience and expectation, the customer will be more inclined to purchase from you and also to return to buy again.

Lights are used to emphasize the product's qualities. If you sell fruit, then lights that intensify the color of the fruit will make it look fresher. Refer to table 3.1 to learn more about the effect the color of lights can have in creating a specific mood.

Color

For many years, color was used to influence people's buying behavior. As with lights, color can create a mood or change emotions. Hotels, restaurants, malls, and clothing stores have used colors to set the customer's mood to align with the product and influence buying.

One research study showed how the color blue increased sales as opposed to red color at the same store. It was found that blue calms people down and makes them feel relaxed, where red makes them feel rushed and under pressure.

	POSITIVE INFLUENCING	NEGATIVE INFLUENCING
RED	Power, Excitement, Strength, Power, Passion, Energy, Youth, Confidence	Anger, Danger, Warning
ORANGE	Confidence, Warmth, Innovation, Friendliness, Energy, Bravery	Frustration, Ignorance, Immaturity
YELLOW	Optimism, Warmth, Happiness, Creativity, Friendliness	Caution, Anxiety, Fear
GREEN	Health, Hope, Nature, Growth, Freshness, Prosperity	Envy, Sickness, Boredom
BLUE	Trust, Loyalty, Dependability, Logic, Serenity, Security	Coldness, Emotionless, Uncaring
PURPLE	Wisdom, Luxury, Wealth, Spirituality, Sophistication, Royalty	Introversion, Decadence, Moodiness
PINK	Imaginative, Passionate, Transformation, Balance, Creativity	Outrageousness, Femininity, Impulsive
BROWN	Serious, Earthiness, Reliability, Authenticity, Warmth, Support	Humorless, Dirty, Sad
BLACK	Sophistication, Security, Power, Authority, Substance	Oppression, Coldness, Menace
WHITE	Cleanness, Clarity, Purity, Simplicity, Freshness	Sterility, Coldness, Isolation

Table 3.1 The effect of color on influencing customers

Music

Music can significantly influence customers' buying behavior. Music can change mood and emotions, direct people to specific products, slow people's movement in a shop, as well as make them eat faster (or slower).

Shopping malls, restaurants, and hotels use music to create an ambiance. Depending on the restaurant, they might play slow romantic music to encourage customers to eat slower and potentially order more expensive wine. On the other hand, steak ranches play louder music that is livelier to encourage customers to eat faster and open space for new customers.

Casinos have used music to their advantage as well. Sounds of winning jackpots continuously fill the room at a casino, and it's all intended to motivate you to gamble. When people hear other people win, they are encouraged to gamble more.

Smell

Aroma is a strong subconscious influencer that motivates customers to stay longer in a shop, buy products they did not intend to buy, or buy more of a specific product. Some companies design their scent that, through research, they found stimulates a smell that will attract their customers. Cinemas ensure that people can smell popcorn even if they aren't close to the cinema, as it will influence them to visit the cinema to watch movies.

There's an old technique (some call it a trick) where real estate agents take freshly baked cookies to the house that they are trying to sell. The fresh smell of cookies makes the potential buyer feel at home and increases the probability of selling the house.

Car salespeople also have a couple of techniques, especially those selling second-hand cars. Spraying the inside of the vehicle with a fresh smelling or new car odor gives the customer a feeling of buying a new car and positively influences their buying decision.

Conclusion

The effectiveness of your selling strategy is its ability to influence your customers to buy your products. The ultimate goal is to sell your products and to retain your customers. Subconscious selling can increase the probability of selling your products. Still, it's important to remember; it's about creating a positive message about your product to encourage potential customers to buy your product above that of your competitor.

Although there are still critics out there who believe these selling techniques are wrong or unethical, it will ultimately depend on your intent and how transparent you are in using subconscious selling techniques.

It's important to ask yourself whether you are doing things in a way that is honest and helpful, and that it will not harm the customer.

CHAPTER 4

EMOTIONAL INTELLIGENT SELLING (EQS)

Introduction

Emotional intelligence (EQ) can be defined as "…the capacity to be aware of, control, and express one's emotions, and to handle interpersonal relationships with good judgment and empathetically". Although this definition still stands true, the world of sales has transformed this definition to include a higher level of emotional functioning. This is especially true considering how technology has disrupted the traditional sales process with the typical sales pitch being irrelevant. A salesperson must learn the skill of emotional control and emotional flexibility, especially trying to sell to a customer who wants quick results, immediate feedback, and has more buying options than ever before.

Having in-depth knowledge about the price, product, and features is critical. But, selling success will only be possible when you can *convince* your customer that your product, price, or features would better speak to their needs than your competitors'. Gone are the days where product or price can give you a significant leading edge above your customers. The only thing that will differentiate between making a sale or not is the ability of the salesperson to sell to a generation that is as knowledgeable about your product as you are (or should be). That ability is what we call Emotional Intelligent Selling.

The critical attributes of Emotional Intelligence in Sales

There are six key attributes that you must possess for you to have the confidence and ability to sell with emotional intelligence. These attributes are essential to influencing your customers to buy your product.

Self-awareness

Having self-awareness means that you are fully aware of your key strengths and weaknesses. It's the ability to interpret your own emotions and behave accordingly. People with high self-awareness understand how their actions and words can influence others, whether positive or negative and can manage these emotions to the best of their situation.

Self-awareness forms the foundation of emotional intelligence. As a salesperson, you should first gain a better understanding of your emotional abilities. Salespeople who are not aware of their emotions won't know how their emotions impact those around them, especially their customers.

Saying the right thing can be wrong if you don't say it right.

You might have the best product knowledge and price, but if the way you communicate it is wrong, the customer may decide to buy the same product elsewhere. There is a range of personality assessments that can assist you in becoming more self-aware like Typersona (www.typersona.com) and Teanamic (www.teanamic.com). Still, the best feedback would be from your colleagues, friends, and sometimes customers.

Self-control

Controlling your emotions is essential in any environment, especially the sales environment where losing self-control can cause you to lose the sale, or even worse, lose the customer. Self-control is about controlling emotional reactions without your emotions impacting your relationships with others. People with high self-control will not overreact to situations or lose their temper when a customer upsets them.

Salespeople must control their emotions at all times and in all situations. Salespeople who get upset quickly or respond to a customer without thinking it through will alienate customers so that they won't have to deal with these negative emotions. Self-control is especially important when the customer objects to something the salesperson said, or if a customer is not interested in a deal the salesperson worked on for a long time. A lack of self-control triggers negative emotions and usually comes out as:

- Anger
- Forceful
- Dominant
- Arrogant
- Fear
- Detachment

Robert Hogan introduced the Hogan Development Survey (HDS) that describes the dark side of the personality, which is losing emotional control in times of increased stress and can disrupt relationships, damage reputations, and derail peoples' chances of success. Salespeople must learn to manage their emotions and control emotional outbursts, whether internal or external.

Empathy

Empathy is the emotional ability to put oneself in other peoples' shoes to understand how they feel about something and appropriately respond to it. Salespeople with high empathy skills can see the problem or need from their customers' point of view and respond with the most appropriate advice. It is crucial to remember that every person reason differently, they think differently about their problems, their perspective is different, and all these differences are where empathy comes in. The salesperson can see the problem from the customer's perspective. This is when the customer will say, "He truly understands my needs".

Sometimes, salespeople may come across as aggressive and pushy just to make the sale. Customers pick up on this and will interpret this as the salesperson being unempathetic. However, the flip side is also true. If a salesperson cares so much about the customer's problems and becomes hyperempathetic, the salesperson might be less concerned about the sale but instead helping the customer.

Adaptability (flexing behavior)

Adaptability is vital in situations or environments with a lot of change. Adapting to something means that you have to adjust or flex your emotions to suit that of the situation or environment. People who struggle to adapt might find it very difficult to cope in sales positions, especially in the fast-changing world of sales and customers.

Salespeople can find themselves being rigid, especially with fixed pricing, and they may feel they don't have any room to negotiate. When they get used to working in this type of environment, they become less adaptable and find it challenging to sell different products to different customers. They will also find it challenging to deal with customers who regularly change their minds. If self-control is low, they might react in an angry or frustrated manner which will deter the customer from buying a product from you. Being adaptable can be quite challenging, especially if you have a personality style that needs predictability and to work in a highly compliant environment. However, it is still critical to develop adaptability to function better in sales environments.

Optimism

People want to buy from optimistic people. Optimistic people see the positive side of life and are always willing to help others and make them see the good in life. Optimistic salespeople sell easier because they believe in what they are doing, believe in their product, and believe in themselves.

Salespeople who are optimistic attract customers, while pessimistic salespeople push customers away. Optimism will also help salespeople deal with rejection easier. If a customer rejects the deal, the optimistic salesperson will look for the next customer who will be interested in their product.

It is essential to understand that optimism is not happiness. Happiness is a short-term mood that can be influenced by a simple change in the environment, where optimism should stay relatively constant.

Optimism is the fuel that drives success

Assertiveness

Assertiveness means being able to stand up for your own or other people's rights in a calm, constructive, and positive way. Sometimes, salespeople are described as being overly assertive. However, assertiveness on the wrong side of the scale can be aggressiveness or shyness.

Shy   **Assertive**   **Aggressive**

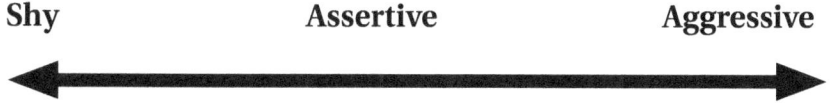

Salespeople should have excellent assertiveness skills. Customers who perceive you as shy might think your confidence is low because you don't believe in your product. The flip side is also true, if the salesperson pushes too hard to make a sale and the sale is all about them, the customer might even walk away because *their* needs were not met.

Salespeople must learn to practice assertiveness so that customers can see their confidence and belief in the product they are selling.

Emotional Intelligent Communication

A salesperson who cannot communicate, cannot sell. Communication is the most critical attribute for a salesperson. Emotional intelligent communication is even more significant because it adds the dimension of emotions to the discussion. One can easily be an effective communicator, but communicating with EQ will make you an interpersonal communicator, and customers prefer to interact with salespeople who are more sincere in their communication.

Communication, at its most basic level, consists of sending and receiving a message. Emotional intelligent communication means the conditioned sending and receiving of a message so that the receiver can understand the intended message. This will not just enable the receiver to know *what* to reply, but *how* to respond. A lot of content in a message can be misunderstood if the receiver misinterprets the intent behind the message.

Asking questions and probing

Asking relevant questions is a critical phase in the communication process. Asking questions is not just about getting an answer but understanding the context, emotion, and involvement in the response. A salesperson must always ask questions and probe, not only for answers but to get to know their customers better.

The asking and probing phase is essential because the wrong question at the wrong time, or the right question in the wrong way, may give you the wrong answer. Probing the wrong answer will cause the customer to think you don't understand their needs, and they will not be interested in buying your product. Always remember, customers with an emotional connection with a product will be willing to pay a premium. You can create that emotional connection by merely asking and probing the customer in an emotional intelligent way.

Salespeople sometimes lose the sale because they are afraid to ask questions. They are worried that they may be rejected if they ask for personal or sensitive information that could help sell the product. The customer will sense your fear and might also interpret it as a lack of confidence, or that you're not sure what their needs are. Your fear will show in your physiology with your voice pitch, pace, and tone changing. You will find yourself speaking with a higher tone, at a much faster pace, and sometimes louder than usual. You may even be too anxious to look your customer in the eyes, which strengthens their perception that you are not confident.

Listening

Listening, as with asking the right questions, is vital to understanding what and why the customer wants in your product. It is easy to understand what the customer wants, but with emotional intelligent listening, you can better understand why the customer wants your product. If you know why, you can respond by answering the customer's emotional need for the product, make that connection, and increase the probability of the sale.

Listening with intent will help you better understand your customer, but you have to know what your intent is. If you intend to sell a product, then you will listen only to find an opportunity to talk about the price or to try to close the sale. However, if you intend to satisfy the needs of the customer, then you will put yourself in their shoes and understand what their needs are, thus fulfilling the needs of the customer. Your customer will pick up on your intent, and that will influence their buying decision.

Responding

Responding accurately and appropriately to questions is the downfall to many people, especially for salespeople. It is easy to answer a question, but to respond to a question that is not aligned to the customer's need or responding with the wrong intent may cause your customer to believe that the sale is about you and not about them.

As a salesperson, you must spend a lot of your time learning how to respond assertively but also with empathy. Your customer must know that you are confident in your product, and at the same time, also interested in helping them find the right product.

Remember, you can respond correctly to the question, but your answer might be wrong. It's all about your intention.

Your physiological demeanor when asking questions, listening, and responding.

You must practice the art of asking, listening, and responding to questions. The more you practice, the more confident you will become in your ability to ask relevant questions and respond appropriately. You can practice this by looking at yourself in a mirror while you ask questions and look at your physical demeanor. Do you look confident, do you feel confident, do you sound confident? You can also practice this with a colleague or a friend who can give you feedback on improving your asking techniques. Consider the following when practicing your asking, listening, and responding techniques:

- Are you asking direct questions? Don't ask leading questions or anticipate answers as this will influence your ability to respond appropriately.
- Are you asking pointed questions? Sometimes salespeople ask long-winded questions because they are trying to sell the product while asking the question.
- Are you confident that you know how to respond to your questions? Salespeople sometimes ask questions just for the sake of asking questions, without considering whether they can answer themselves.
- Are you asking relevant questions? Your questions should focus on getting to know the customer as well as their need.
- Do you listen intently? Are you listening to your customer to get to know them, or listening to be ready with an answer?
- Are you looking the customer in their eyes and acknowledging what they are saying? Customers need to know

that you are listening to them only and that you recognize what they are saying and understand their needs.
- Are you asking clarifying questions? Don't always assume you know the customer's needs because you've worked with a similar customer before. Each customer is different, and you must clarify that you clearly understand their needs.
- Are you responding to *their* questions and comments? Your response must be relevant to the questions and comments, and not your preconceived answers.
- Does your body posture reflect your intent? A confident salesperson will stand up straight and speak at a reasonable speed; the tone of their voice will be normal, not too high; you're talking loud enough that your customer can hear you, without shouting, but also not too soft that they can't listen to what you are saying. Eye contact is critical, look your customer in the eyes and respond by nodding your head or saying you understand; stand up straight, hands out of your pockets.
- Have you considered your non-verbal gestures? The use of your hands when you speak or ask questions must not be too much or too little.
- Listen to your "filling words": Sometimes people can't remember the right word and will overuse filling words like "ums" or "so".

The Emotional Buyer vs Buying with emotions

There is a distinct difference between an emotional buyer and someone who buys with emotions. We must understand the difference between an emotional buy vs buying with emotions. One is positive, the other negative; one is rational, and the other is impulsive; the one may be more prone to regret their purchase, where the other will feel good about their purchase. Your responsibility as a salesperson is to distinguish whether your customer is an emotional buyer or a customer buying with emotions. Emotions always play the most significant part of buying. It is the salesperson who can and will distinguish between the two and who will adapt their sales approach and who will be better at sales.

> *"People do not buy goods & services. They buy relations, stories, and magic."*
>
> **— Seth Godin**

Selling to an emotional buyer might be easy because they don't think about it rationally and tend to make an impulsive buy. However, will this be a returning customer? Will they return if they regret their purchase and feel that you didn't allow them to think about the decision rationally? Emotional buyers are influenced by external stimuli like influences, creative marketing, and salespeople. Salespeople can influence customers to buy using envy, pride, vanity, sentiment, arrogance, and entertainment as a buying criterion. They influence customers to buy impulsively before they can think about whether they need this product or if the product is worth buying. A lot of salespeople have high sales figures with this approach. These techniques also relate to what we discussed in Chapter 3 on subconscious selling, where the customer is influenced to buy something they might not need, but has been *strategically* advertised or placed in a store to influence the sale. We are not saying that emotional buyers should be ignored or refused as customers. Still, it is vital that as salespeople, we do as much as possible to ensure our customers' decision to buy is made with enough relevant information to justify the purchase.

> "Comfort. Acceptance. Power. Freedom. Control. Love. We are all longing to find satisfaction for our intangible desires. If you can provide a payoff for your prospects' unspoken needs, you will find yourself handsomely rewarded."
>
> **— Chris Goward, Author, You Should Test That!**

As mentioned earlier, buying with emotions is different from emotional buying. All buying decisions are based on emotions. Information hardly sells, if it sells at all. If that information aligns with an emotion, then it will sell. Zig Ziglar once said that "People don't buy for logical reasons, they buy for emotional reasons". Even though emotion is what drives the buying behaviors, the conscious mind still plays a part in the final decision-making process.

Michael Harris wrote:

> "I discovered that people do not decide emotionally. The decision to buy is made subconsciously, and these subconscious decisions are based on a deeply empirical mental processing system that follows a logic of its own. Our subconscious/intuitive decision to buy is then communicated to the conscious mind via an emotion. The conscious mind then searches for rational reasons, and that's how we complete the circle: We justify our emotional signals to buy with logical reasons".

It summarizes the most significant difference between emotional buying and buying with emotions. Buying with emotions involves a conscious decision, whereas emotional buying is usually impulsive without the necessary mental processing to justify the decision. Research done by Professor Gerald Zaltman at the Harvard Business School found that 95% of our purchase decisions take place subconsciously. And, according to Harris, these subconscious decisions are communicated to our conscious mind via emotions. For the customer, this is good news, knowing that most of their choices will have a rational decision-making process, and not all are emotional decisions. But how does this change things for salespeople?

If a customer uses their emotions to influence their conscious decision to buy, the salesperson must also use emotions to convince the customer. We've discussed in Chapter 3 how salespeople can subliminally influence customers to buy, that is, influence the subconscious, which sends an emotion to the conscious mind to buy a product. However, most of the time, salespeople do not have access, knowledge, or the understanding to use subconscious selling techniques and must trust their emotional intelligence to do the selling. And that's why it is so important for salespeople to develop their emotional intelligence; it's the *intelligent use of emotions* that may influence your customer to buy from you.

Dealing with a demanding customer

There's just no escaping this; you will always have that one customer, the one customer who's the main character in all your nightmare stories, the customer you wish you never met, that *demanding* customer. The interesting thing is, we all know difficult people because we all know ourselves. They have always been there, and they will always be there, so we can either fear them or learn how to deal with them, and just maybe, turn a difficult person into a returning customer.

There are numerous types of demanding customers that can include everything from angry customers to impatient customers; some are very demanding where others are more indecisive. As a salesperson, you will have to deal with them and find a way to fulfill their needs, regardless of the emotion.

Steps to deal with demanding customers:

1. Control your own emotions: Make sure you don't react to their emotional state and show them that you are willing to help them;
2. Listen with intent: Allow your customer to vent and to get their frustrations out. Sometimes it's not even the product, but previous bad service they received;
3. Repeat their concerns back to them: Make sure they know that you understand their concerns;
4. Apologize and offer solutions: Whether it was terrible customer service or the product didn't do what it was supposed to do, apologize, and immediately offer solutions to rectify it. Do not blame anyone when you apologize or talk bad about the product or customer service. Do not apologize for the things you didn't do wrong, because it will only give them a reason to complain more. Keep it objective and to the point;
5. Implement a solution: After you have agreed on a solution, implement or deliver this as soon as possible.
6. Ask for feedback: Always ask the customer if the solution fulfills their needs and if you can help in any other way. Show that you care, even after you have solved their problem.

More tips for dealing with demanding customers:

EMOTION	DESCRIPTION	YOUR RESPONSE
DEMANDING	Believes he knows what he wants and will require that you deliver, even if it is out of your control	Ensure him that you understand his need; Explain your product and be clear about the features and be honest as to whether it will fulfill his needs
IMPULSIVE	Always ready to buy, might miss important details	Explain your product very briefly but be specific; If he is clear about his need and the product, try and make the purchase as quick and easy as possible
AGGRESSIVE	Can be loud and attacking, feels his need is more important	Don't argue; Don't get emotional; Show alternatives; Stay calm
DOUBTS EVERYTHING	Can be seen as a pessimist and not trusting you or the product	Be empathetic; Ask relevant questions; Be visible with your solutions (show how it works)

Why are some customers demanding?

There are thousands of reasons why customers are demanding, but the main reason is that their needs are not met. This need can be conscious or unconscious, and it's the salespersons' responsibility to understand this need before they can offer their services or products.

Conscious vs unconscious need

The first thing we have to realize is that there will always be a need. However, this need can be a conscious need or an unconscious need. A conscious need is when the customer knows what they need, maybe not exactly what it is, but they know they do have a need. The unconscious need is when the customer doesn't know that they need something, yet it doesn't take the need away or make it easier to fulfill. Just because a customer knows what their needs are doesn't mean it's easier to meet, because the mere fact that they know what they need means that they won't accept anything else.

The customer with a conscious need may be demanding because a salesperson has not taken the time to understand what their needs are. The flip side of it is that the customer knows what their needs are, but finds it difficult to explain to the salesperson, and that creates frustration for both the customer and the salesperson. This is where the salesperson must use their emotional intelligence, more specifically empathy and patience, to ask the right questions, in the right way, to understand the need better. The salesperson should not try to sell a product's features to this customer and hope it will fulfill their needs, but instead, offer solutions and possibilities to help this customer. If you can find the solution, you can work backward to find the product that will provide the solution. It is important to remember with all customers that you never prescribe or lead the customer to a solution that will work in your view, but rather advise the customer on potential solutions and let them decide what will work for them.

The customer with the unconscious need might be a bit trickier to sell to because neither the customer nor you know what the need is. The customer might not even realize they need something.

> "Some people say, 'Give the customers what they want.' But that's not my approach. Our job is to figure out what they're going to want before they do. I think Henry Ford once said, 'If I'd asked customers what they wanted, they would have told me, 'A faster horse!' People don't know what they want until you show it to them. That's why I never rely on market research. Our task is to read things that are not yet on the page."
>
> **— Steve Jobs**

The unconscious need is not necessarily an *unknown* need for a product that doesn't exist yet. As an example, say a customer may have a conscious need to buy a new car, but an unconscious need to solve their social status. Purchasing a new vehicle might satisfy their conscious need, but it won't necessarily meet their unconscious needs. As a salesperson, if you know their unconscious need, you can recommend a car that will give them "social status". This will satisfy the unconscious need and reduce the possibility of the customer becoming difficult because you're just trying to sell them a car.

It's not about saving the world or solving all the unknown problems, but rather to know your products well enough that you can see potential solutions for your customers before the need negatively impacts them, and they become that problematic customer.

> "Onions have layers. Ogres have layers... You get it? We both have layers."
>
> **— Schrek**

Handling Objections

In 350 BC, Aristotle wrote: *"Anyone can become angry – that's easy. But to be angry with the right person to the right degree, at the right time for the right purpose and in the right way – that is not easy."*

Most customers will have sales objections or reasons they're hesitant to buy a product. Sales objections are unavoidable, and as a salesperson, you first need to understand why they objected and secondly, know how to deal with it from an internal and external perspective.

Why do customers object?

There are a myriad of reasons why customers object to your offer, and you must understand why. When you know why they're not interested in your product, it will give you valuable information on what precisely their objection or concern might be. Whether it's the product or the customer, it may be that they are not ready to buy, or the product is too expensive. When you know why they rejected the offer, you can actively put steps in place to either help this customer differently or be better equipped to help future customers.

Some common causes of why customers object:

1. Lack of knowledge: They don't know enough, so they're not ready to buy.
2. Product-specific concern: The product is too expensive.
3. They're fishing: They are not interested in buying, they are only gathering information, pretending to be interested in buying.
4. Skewed Perception: What they were told previously was not accurate, so customers assume the same is true about your product.

Whatever their reason, the better you understand their concerns, the better you can support them in the future.

Handling objections internally

When a prospective customer is not interested in your product, it can be challenging to deal with this rejection, especially if it happens a few times. The first response is usually to internalize it and to take it personally; however, it is essential to realize that most of the time it has to do with the customer or the product. To handle objections internally, you have to learn to have resilience and not to lose hope. Most salespeople fail because the way they deal with rejection is less effective and they take it too personally. It impacts their self-confidence, and they feel they are not good at anything. But this is where emotional intelligence comes in, helping you handle these objections without it impacting your physical or psychological health. Learn to accept objections and to learn from every experience. The stronger you bounce back, the stronger your next sales approach. Remember, most of the time, customers reject because of *their* own reasons (they can't afford it, they don't associate with it), or they reject the product (preferring a different brand, already own such a product, quality too low, or the price too high).

Handling objections externally

How you handle objections externally will mostly depend on how you handled it internally and that also shows your emotional intelligence. People with high emotional intelligence will cope better with a customer rejecting their products; they are resilient and bounce back and have the confidence to try again. However, people struggling to handle rejection internally will usually express this externally, and this can damage the relationship with the customer as well as the brand and product.

To handle objections externally, you could practice the following techniques:

1. Don't react, respond: The moment you react to a situation, the chances are that it will be emotionally loaded, and you might say the wrong things. Before you do or say anything, gather your thoughts, make sure you professionally respond to the customer;
2. Compose yourself: Do not show the customer that you are upset or angry. It is normal to be disappointed but be careful not to show the customer that you are not happy with their decision and react negatively. Remember, your body language speaks volumes about your internal thoughts than what expressed words could;
3. Thank them regardless: To show gratitude even when they reject your product will show them that you were genuinely interested in solving their needs and not just your own need to sell. Thank them for the time they gave to listen to your pitch, even though they are not interested in the product;
4. Ask for feedback: It's not just about what you ask, but how you ask. If you merely ask the customer why they are not interested in your product, you can expect a straightforward "because I'm not interested" answer. However, if you ask for feedback to better understand how you can serve them better in the future, customers will be more prone to give honest feedback.

Always remember, maybe this person was never a prospect in the first place, so their rejection is empty. You have to learn to identify a genuine prospective customer with a valid need for your product.

Do they like you?

"When it comes right down to it, whatever business you're in, you're in the people business. After all, people prefer to do business with people and companies they find likable."

— **Karen Salmansohn**

Likability has never been one of the focus areas in teaching people to sell. Some say that people don't need to like you to buy from you which, in essence, is true. However, people are attracted to others they can associate with and who they like. You only have 7 seconds to make a first impression, and it's impossible to impress a potential customer with your specialist expertise and how knowledgeable you are about the product within those 7 seconds. Customers usually look for a salesperson they feel they can connect with, who can understand their needs, who they can trust, and someone they like. Research has shown that very likable people are hired and promoted quicker than their "unlikable" counterparts. The same is true in selling. Salespeople who are more likable outsell those who are less likable.

Being likable does not mean everyone wants to connect with you on Facebook and become your best friend.

The Oxford Lexicon defines *likable* as a person who is pleasant, friendly, and easy to like. Likable is not a crystallized personality type or what you are born with, but an attribute of someone who is emotionally mature. If "likability" is the ability to be liked, then you can develop those skills to be better liked. Before you search for a course on likability, it is important to understand the critical descriptors of someone who is likable.

The Cambridge dictionary describes *likable* as someone who is:

- Welcoming
- Cordial
- Agreeable
- Hospitable
- Warm
- Amiable

As you can see, these are attributes that any person can learn and improve. "But", you may ask, "what if I am the only salesperson to sell a specific product in a specific region? I could then be who I want to be, and I don't need others to like me. If they want to buy from me, the customer must be likable". First, if this is your attitude, then you're not a salesperson. Second, being the only person who has a specific product is so rare these days, especially in our world of technology. Third, know that competition is on its way, then customers will automatically take their business to the new kid on the block who can deliver better customer service.

Likability should not be a smokescreen you use to fool customers into thinking you are likable. Authenticity goes hand in hand with being likable. Customers will immediately pick up when you are not authentic, and that will cause them to lose trust in you and the product, even before they've met you.

Likeability, in short, is this. Smile when you greet people, be friendly and respectful, put their needs first, and help wherever you can.

Conclusion

Research has shown that Emotional intelligence accounts for 40% of performance[2]. PepsiCo found that executives selected

---

2 http://www.handbagsintheboardroom.com/number-one-predictor-success-eq/

for EQ competencies generated 10% more productivity, and at L'Oreal, sales managers with advanced emotional intelligence brought in $2.5 million more in sales. Research conducted by The Carnegie Institute of Technology showed that 85% of financial success was due to humanistic skills, personality, and ability to communicate, negotiate, and lead. Only 15% was because of their technical ability.

EQ is proven to be a significant differentiator in work performance and success, especially sales success. It goes without saying that if you want to improve your sales ability, you must start with EQ development. Having advanced EQ skills will help you better understand your customers, whether it's a satisfied customer or a demanding customer, a customer knowing what their needs are, or a customer still trying to see if they have a need.

Your career success starts with you, and how well you understand yourself and your ability to understand others.

CHAPTER 5

SELLING AND BUYING PERSONALITIES

Introduction

In Chapter 4, we discussed the importance of emotional intelligence in building rapport, effectively interacting with people, and how emotions drive behavior. In the same manner, your personality type also influences your behavioral style and values. Although we are all unique, human beings share specific characteristics that enable us to group people in different personality types. It is, however, essential to understand that the purpose of grouping people into different personality types is not to *box* people, but rather to identify behavioral characteristics that are common or similar between them. On the most basic level, we get extroverts and introverts. Extroverts prefer working in an environment where they can continuously interact with others, whereas introverts prefer more independent work. It is also important to mention that personality preferences are not abilities and also do not limit behavior. It is an individual's preference to work in a particular environment, but it does not mean they cannot work in other types of environments.

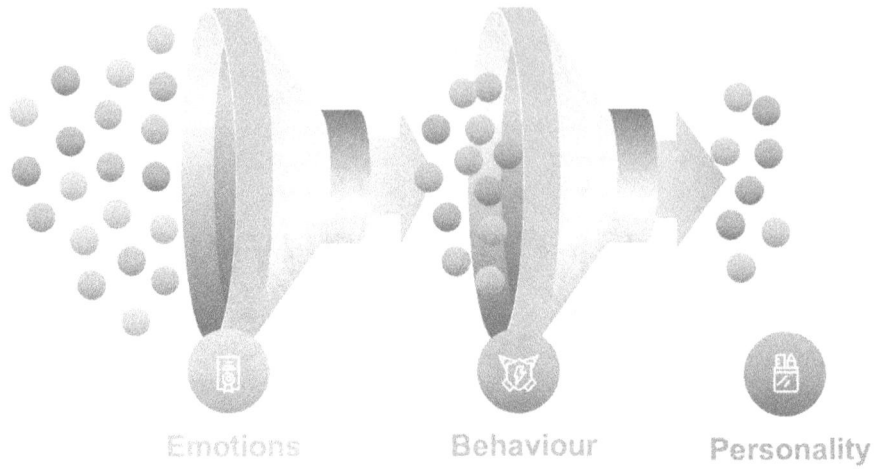

Fluid Behaviour

The *fluid* terminology originally stems from describing intelligence. Fluid intelligence refers to the ability to reason and solve problems in unique and novel situations. In contrast, crystallized intelligence refers to the ability to use the knowledge acquired through prior learning or experience. Thus, fluid is an *adapting* state, and crystallized a *permanent* state. Fluid behavior then describes how people adapt their behavior to different environments and situations. The difference between fluid behavior and emotional intelligence is that emotional intelligence is the *ability* to adjust behavior, whereas fluid behavior is *how* we adapt our behavior. In other words, fluid behavior is dependent on emotional intelligence. People with enhanced emotional intelligence abilities will find adapting to different environments easier, thus enabling people to respond and behave differently whenever the environment or situation demands it. Adapting behavior is also known as flexing, which will be discussed later on in this chapter.

Customers are attracted to people who think and communicate like them. As mentioned before, we are all unique, and our responses to different situations might be different. This chapter will look at different personality types and behavioral styles and how each type must adapt to similar or other types depending on the situation.

Personality Types

In the world of psychology, we get an array of personality and behavior type assessments. There are numerous online assessments that you can take to determine your personality type and style, which will help you to understand yourself better. Websites like www.teanamic.com and www.typersona.com offer different personality type assessments used to learn more about your preferred style of thinking, your values, and team role.

Some of the best-known personality assessments are based on the Jung typology theory. According to Carl G. Jung's theory of psychological types, people are characterized by their preference of general attitude. The Myers Briggs Type Inventory (MBTI) and the Typersona assessment both offer the individual better insights into their personality types as initially theorized by Jung.

In the early 1920s, William Moulton Marston created the DISC model for emotions and behavior. In 1924, he first studied the concepts of *will* and a person's sense of power and their effect on personality and human behavior. DISC, like the Typersona, provides us with a basic overview of our behavioral styles and how fluid behavior comes into effect in different environments. The DISC model is also used in other types of personality assessments, like the Insights tests that assigned colors to the four DISC behavior types.

This chapter focuses mainly on the DISC model and how you can use it to understand better your selling behavior, as well as your customers' buying behavior. We will also look at different techniques that you can use to flex your behavior to influence them better to buy your products.

Before continuing with this chapter, we would like to recommend that you complete AssessmentHouse's DISC assessment available for free at: http://www.assessmenthouse.com/disc

Overview of the DISC model

Marston explained that people illustrate their emotions using four types. The following table shows the DISC model and how it is used in testing:

	Marston's theory	Personal Profile Analysis (PPA)®	DISC Indicator Profile (DIP)®	Insights®
D	Dominance	Dominance	Drive	Red
I	Inducement	Influence	Interaction	Yellow
S	Submission	Steadiness	Stability	Green
C	Compliance	Compliance	Conscientiousness	Blue

Regardless of the assessment methodology you are using; it can all be applied to the selling and buying behavior model we discuss in this chapter.

It is important to note that there are no good or bad profiles. The profiles only suggest a preference for individual behavioral styles and understanding your own style will give you a better opportunity to build a relationship with your customer using your strengths.

D
- Determined
- Confident
- Direct
- Decisive
- Assertive
- Focused
- Demanding
- Competitive

People who have both outgoing and task-oriented traits often exhibit dominant and direct behaviours. They usually focus on results, problem-solving, and the bottom-line.

I
- Interactive
- Engaging
- Enthusiastic
- Excited
- Influential
- Sociable
- Persuasive
- Demonstrative

People who have both outgoing and people-oriented traits often exhibit inspiring and interactive behaviours. They usually focus on interacting with people, having fun, and creating excitement.

S
- Stability
- Security
- Predictablility
- Supportive
- Calm
- Routine
- Relaxed
- Steady

People who have both reserved and people-oriented traits often exhibit supportive and steady behaviours. They usually focus on preserving relationships and on creating or maintain peace. harmony.

C
- Compliant
- Conscientious
- Details
- Cautious
- Precise
- Consistent
- Objective
- Analytical

People who have both reserved and task-oriented traits often exhibit cautious and careful behaviour. They usually focus on facts, rules and correctness.

Selling and Buying Styles

Table 5.1 illustrates the different selling and buying styles based on the DISC model. Please refer to your DISC report and use the table below to learn more about your selling style and your customers' buying style.

Drive

Selling Style (Salesperson)	Buying Style (Customer)
Confident and assertive, they get to the point, and the main focus is on selling without too much explaining. They are very ambitious and competitive and will usually try to get the best deal for themselves. They are target driven, so expect this person to be quite forceful to get the deal done.	They know what they want and don't need too much information. They are not interested in a long-winded sales pitch. They are very competitive and will push to get the best deal for themselves. They are also assertive and will let the salesperson know if they don't agree with anything.
Others might think this person is too aggressive and focuses more on closing the deal than influencing the customer to buy. Others might also see them as too direct and not concerned about their feelings.	Salespeople might perceive this person as too pushy or demanding, always wanting their products urgently. Others may also find it challenging to sell to this person because they can be insensitive.

Interaction

Selling Style (Salesperson)	Buying Style (Customer)
They like to network and socialize; they sell using their persuasiveness and negotiation skills. They want to talk through the options available and will prefer to discuss and demonstrate the product features. They will try to find a win-win solution.	They like to have informal discussions with the salesperson and will probably focus on building a trusting relationship before they will buy. They won't argue too much if they don't agree and will value the relationship more than the money they have to pay for a product.
Others might see them as too talkative and more focused on the relationship than the product. Customers might get frustrated with them because they want to talk and interact more than just getting to the point and selling the product.	Salespeople might find it challenging to discuss technical information with this customer because the customer is more interested in talking than analyzing. Salespeople might find these customers to be more focused on building a lasting relationship than just buying the product and moving on.

Stability

Selling Style (Salesperson)	Buying Style (Customer)
They like to work in predictable environments where they can be assured of their selling potential. They prefer routine-based selling where they can be more office-based than being out on the road doing cold selling. Others might find them to be too rigid in their approach and might push potential customers away because they are not flexible in their approach. They might also prefer to work at a slower pace that will frustrate customers who need a quick turnaround.	They can be predictable in their buying behavior, usually settling for the known products. They want salespeople to explain things at a steady pace, not rushing the process. They prefer constant feedback from the salesperson through the entire selling process. Others might perceive them to be too rigid, and salespeople might find it challenging to sell a new concept to them. Salespeople might find them to be overly sensitive under pressure and pushing back any last-minute sales.

Conscientiousness

Selling Style (Salesperson)	Buying Style (Customer)
They are very organized and will sell using a clearly outlined process that provides them with clear guidelines and instructions on how to sell. They are very thorough in their selling and will tend to explain the features in much detail. Customers might find them to be too detailed and too focused on the features of the product rather than on the solution. Others might also find them quite cold in their presentations because their focus is more on the facts than opinions/inputs from others.	They want a lot of detailed information about the product before they consider buying it. They tend to ask a lot of clarifying questions and have a great need for facts. They want to think and reason through their options to ensure they know what they are buying. Salespeople might find them to be too focused on the facts and might miss the opportunities the product may provide. They may also be too interested in the sales process and that the salesperson carefully guides them through the entire process, one step at a time.

Table 5.1 Selling and Buying Behavioral Styles

DISC Flexing

Flexing behavior means adapting your behavior styles to that of your customers. Flexing behavior requires a certain level of emotional intelligence, where higher emotional intelligence will support better flexing.

Flexing the D

Your Style	Customer Style	How to flex
D	D	Little to no flexing necessary. Your strongest behavioral type matches that of your customer. Like your profile, your customer wants to finalize the deal as quickly as you do. Make sure, however, that you still provide them with enough information to make an informed decision.
D	I	You should be less demanding and more persuasive. Be careful not to force the sale before you've built a trusting relationship with your customers. Be assertive but also empathetic; your customer wants to be assured that you have heard them and want to provide them with a solution.
D	S	Be sure to listen more and explain things in such a way that will make sense. Explain your ideas in such a way that they will clearly understand your intentions. Make sure that you communicate more and provide regular feedback.
D	C	Don't push for the sale; explain things in more detail until the customer has all the relevant information. Do not rush them through the information but rather discuss each topic individually. Do not skip any steps in the selling process; they want to plan and follow a step-by-step procedure.

Flexing the I

Your Style	Customer style	How to flex
I	D	Do not talk too much before getting to the point. Keep your introduction concise and only provide customers with the necessary information for them to decide. Don't ask too many questions about their needs, listen intently, and provide solutions asap.
I	I	Little to no flexing necessary. Your strongest behavioral type matches that of your customer. Like you, the customer wants to have informal discussions and build rapport before you try and sell anything. Just make sure that you do sell your product and not get lost in all the chats.
I	S	Don't try to persuade the customer to buy before you've built a relationship and they can trust you. Provide regular feedback and provide timelines where possible. Don't try to sell your ideas to them but explain the solutions and how it will resolve their needs.
I	C	Communicate more factual than general information. Document all your discussions to ensure your customer can go back and review what was discussed. Do not influence them with your persona but convince them with facts. Make sure your message flows in an organized manner.

Flexing the S

Your Style	Customer style	How to flex
S	D	Do not focus too much on providing lots of information, give them the most important facts, then move on with the process. Be less concerned with building long-lasting relationships, but rather focus on providing the customer with a solution. The customer wants quick results, so try to be less thorough in your presentation.
	I	Build rapport and find commonalities before trying to sell a product. Provide regular feedback and keep it informal. Your customer will trust you quickly; don't try too hard to build a relationship forcing your customer to depend on you.
	S	Little to no flexing necessary. Your strongest behavioral type matches that of your customer. Like your profile, your customer also wants to build trusting relationships and work at a steady pace.
	C	Do not expect your customer to follow your processes. Your need for predictability may support your customer to plan and organize accordingly. Provide enough technical/practical information.

Flexing the C

Your Style	Customer style	How to flex
C	D	Summarize your information into more concise and to the point information. Share fewer details and focus more on efficiencies. Don't over-organize a meeting; keep it short and flexible.
	I	Do not try to convince them with too many facts or details. They prefer to talk about things rather than read long documents. Allow your customer to talk more about their needs and come up with solutions with them.
	S	Make sure when you plan and organize something that it will provide your customer with a clear sense of direction and be specific about what is required. Communicate in advance if the plan needs to change so that your customer can prepare.
	C	Little to no flexing necessary. Your strongest behavioral type matches that of your customer. Like your profile, both of you require detailed information and quality work.

Your profile may indicate that your D and I are both strong, or your I and C are strong. It is also possible that your I and S and C are strong. Whichever style is your strong preference, use the above table and learn how you can flex your behavior to build better rapport with your customers and influence them to buy your products.

Determine your customer's DISC profile (without a test)

It's not always, if ever, possible to assess all your customers to understand their DISC profile for you to know how you must flex your behavior to better adapt to them. However, there are some behavioral characteristics and non-verbal gestures that you can look out for when you meet a new (or existing) customer. The more you learn and practice these, the better you will become at reading your customer's behavior.

You can also download this reference guide from https://assessmenthouse.com/discmyclient.pdf

Style	Characteristics
D	<ul><li>They ask direct questions</li><li>They make a lot of direct eye contact</li><li>They might interrupt you a lot while you're talking</li><li>They can come across as very confident, even arrogant</li><li>They don't listen well, can be distracted</li><li>They want a solution or the product immediately</li><li>They are quite expressive, both verbally and nonverbally</li><li>They have a firm handshake</li><li>They will choose performance over safety</li></ul>

I
- They will make small talk
- They tend to be loud
- They will show a lot of excitement and enthusiasm
- They will be very friendly
- They are very expressive, verbally and nonverbally
- They will seek attention
- They are usually very informal
- They will make jokes
- They respond more emotionally than logically
- Will ask basic questions and allow you to talk most of the time

S
- They are very good at listening, so expect them to be somewhat reserved
- They will be very concerned about the safety of the product
- They will choose safety over performance
- They will show sincere appreciation
- They have a calm demeanor
- They will be humble
- They might be a bit indecisive
- They will ask for clear instructions on how to proceed with something

C
- They will ask a lot of "how" questions
- They will be very concerned with the compliance of the product
- They need a lot of facts
- They will spot small mistakes on paper or product damages
- They will ask a lot of facts about the product
- They will be quite skeptical
- They won't show a lot of emotion
- They don't ask vague or general information
- They will always want to double-check with you

Conclusion

People have unique personalities; however, we all share similar behavioral characteristics. People also interact easier and build trust with those who are similar or share the same behavioral attributes. In understanding your personality style and behavioral characteristics and learning how to interact with different customers with their unique behavioral traits, you increase the possibility of building quicker and better rapport with them. When your customers feel they can easily interact with you, they will trust your advice and be more inclined to buy from you.

It is important to remember; you are trying to sell your product to a customer. It is your responsibility to build rapport with your customer, which means you may have to adapt your behavior to suit your customers.

CHAPTER 6

THE SALES EQUATION

Introduction

Selling is one of the oldest professions in the world. Whether it was selling for money or the exchange of goods, sales have been around since almost the beginning of time. It was also then that the sales formula was introduced, although somewhat primitive. The Ford Motor Company introduced the famous "Science of Selling" and included the message "*sell the vehicle according to the shape of the prospect's head. High foreheads leave room for larger development and indicate people who are less likely to resist new ideas*" in their sales training. This, in itself, had its own sales formula for success and unbeknown then, became the foundation of the sales formula.

The sales function in many organizations has seen numerous transformations and over time, became one of the most critical strategic drivers of organizations. Almost all organizations have a sales strategy built on a sales plan that outlines the organization's sales activities. In our fast-moving world, the sales strategy must be reviewed more often than anything else in an organization to ensure it is still aligned to the business strategy and enabling the business to be competitive in their market. In the modern world of business, the sales strategy that worked yesterday will be outdated today and will be a sales risk tomorrow.

It is important to note that there is no *generic* sales formula that will work for your organization. Even though this might have been true in the past, being competitive today and staying ahead of your competition means that your sales formula must be unique to your organization, your product, and also to you, the salesperson. Some guiding principles are used in all sales formulas, but the weight of each factor within the formula will depend on your product and ideal customer. As a foundation, your sales formula might look something like this:

$$SS = (pQ \times cp)^b$$

Sales Success = (product Intelligence x customer profile)[brand]

At the most basic level of this formula, having an in-depth knowledge of your product and knowing who your ideal customer is, should lead to sales success. Product and customer knowledge are the foundation of this formula, providing the starting point for your organization-specific sales formula.

Product Knowledge (pQ)

$$pQ = (spc + tra + pe)$$

Product Intelligence = (salesperson competence + training + performance enablement)

Product intelligence, or pQ, is one of the most critical factors in selling. A salesperson with limited knowledge of the products' features, attributes, and benefits will not be successful at selling. Product intelligence is not about the product per se but on the capabilities of the salesperson. Organizations spend a lot of time and money on product training, believing that the salesperson will be able to sell once they know everything about the product. However, the training will only be beneficial and make a difference if they recruit salespeople with the most appropriate behavioral and cognitive attributes necessary to sell that *specific product*.

Recruiting competent salespeople

Recruiting competent salespeople is the first important step in building a successful sales team. It is important to note that a successful car salesperson will not necessarily be successful in selling boats, hence the importance of understanding your product as well as your ideal customer, to recruit the most appropriate salesperson.

Research has shown that there are some common behavioral attributes and values that most salespeople share. We discussed these attributes in chapter 1, and these attributes must be considered when you recruit salespeople. These attributes can be measured using reliable psychometric assessments and competency-based interviews.

Cognitive agility was also found to predict success and should be used when searching for your next salesperson. Cognitive agility is defined as the ability to adapt to different situations and environments, having mental flexibility, and the ability to learn new information quickly.

Sales training

We've discussed earlier how organizations spend time and money training salespeople on the products they have to sell. However, sales training should include more relevant learning outcomes than merely knowing the product. Sales training should also be an on-going process, rather than a once-off session at induction.

Product training is critical for any person who wants to be successful in sales. But product training encompasses more than just teaching the salesperson *what* the product is, *how* it is used, and *how* it is priced. To understand your product, you must understand the need your product is filling in the market. You must understand who the target market is and how to approach this target market. An in-depth analysis of the target market is critical, especially if you have products with different target markets. Salespeople must understand how to approach different target markets and also advise potential customers about the most suitable product for their needs. To understand the need, salespeople must understand the market and which product is more appropriate. It is also important that salespeople keep learning about the product. Regular product-related knowledge assessments can measure if your salespeople are continually growing in your business.

The Sales Process, discussed in chapter 7, is also vitally important, and the salesperson must understand how to utilize the sales process to ensure they guide the customer through each phase of the process. Salespeople may rush the sales process to make the sale but lose the customer because they didn't explain the product well enough or consider payment options. Customers may not know your product well enough to make an informed decision, and more input from the salesperson will be required to inform the potential customer. However, some customers may be very familiar with your product and will be more interested in discussing the best deal, rather than the product. The sales process should be adapted to the target market and never rushed.

Selling behavior, as discussed in chapter 5, refers to the salesperson's selling style. Training programs may focus too much on how customers buy products, but it hardly ever includes the salesperson's selling style and behavior. The salesperson must adjust their selling style to the buying style of the customer. Salespeople may prefer to demonstrate a product by inviting the customer to experience the product before they share any product-specific information. In contrast, other salespeople prefer to explain a product first before demonstrating it to a customer. Salespeople may also prefer to be more focused on doing a need analysis where they ask a lot of questions before explaining or demonstrating any products. Although there is no right or wrong selling style, the salesperson must understand their styles and adapt to the customers' buying behavior.

We also learned in chapter 5 that customers have different buying styles and behaviors. Understanding your target market and their specific buying styles and behavior is critical because a salesperson can lose a deal if they don't adapt to each customer's buying style. In the modern world, and especially the younger generations, potential customers usually have most, if not all, of the available product information. Thus, when they meet the salesperson, they might even have more information than the salesperson and won't need a salesperson to explain or demonstrate the products. Salespeople selling cars find themselves in an industry where the younger generation is less interested in test driving a car, but more interested in price or other specifications. They can also do most of the buying process online without the need for a salesperson. They only meet the salesperson when they take delivery of their new car.

As previously discussed, understanding your product is vital. However, understanding your competitors' products is critical. Your selling strategy should not only focus on your products' strengths but also your competitors' weaknesses.

Competitor ignorance = Customer confusion

Ignoring your competitors' products, especially how they compete with your products, may cause a potential customer to buy your competitors' products instead if they can make a better comparison and convince customers that their products are superior to yours. Knowing your competitors' products will empower you to sell your products' strengths and how they are better than your competitors' products. It is crucial to remember that knowing your strengths and your competitors' weaknesses does not mean badmouthing your competitor or their products. You want to win your customer because they want your product, not because it's option two.

Performance Enablement

Most people, except HR, cringe by merely thinking about performance management. Research indicates that over 70% of all large companies are reviewing their performance management strategy. Some companies like General Electric, Adobe, and Deloitte ditched their performance review processes and invested in performance enablement practices like check-in sessions, informal *touchpoints*, and one-on-one development discussions. Also, more importantly, these sessions are held more regularly, some even weekly, but most importantly, it's informal and focused on the individuals' strengths and potential areas of development. The potential development areas are addressed almost in real-time to ensure it doesn't significantly impact performance. We have to stop trying to manage performance, which is about "controlling and making decisions," without maximizing performance. When we manage performance, we stifle employees' ability to be their best and grow.

Measuring performance has always been one of the most challenging practices in any business, mainly because of its subjectivity, lack of clear measuring standards, and the impact of leadership on actual performance. Measuring performance in the sales industry is based on targets and goals; i.e. how many products were sold compared to the sales targets. There are numerous scientific ways of determining targets and sales goals. However, these targets are usually based on inputs and outputs, and hardly ever consider the impact of sales managers and other managers that can impact individual performance. Creating a sales culture is as crucial as training people to sell. Performance management should instead change to performance enablement, where a large part of sales managers' responsibility is to enable their team to perform, instead of only measuring actual performance. A proactive approach where sales performance is cultivated through a conducive sales culture, with managers taking an individual interest in each salesperson's strengths and sales style, will enable salespeople to perform.

If one is to consider the behavioral attributes that predict sales success, it only makes sense that the culture should enable salespeople to behave in such a way that it will motivate them to perform. Creating an environment where salespeople are enthusiastic and have a passion for your product and brand will enable a performance-driven culture. Salespeople are generally curious, and they want to learn more, thus ensuring a learning culture where salespeople can learn new things, inspiring them to commit to your business and sell because they believe in your brand and products. This will contribute to your performance enabled culture.

Customer Profile

$$cp = (dg + gg + sg + pg + eg + g)$$

customer profile = (demographic + geographic + sociographic + psychographic + e-graphic + generations)

Who is your ideal customer? Have you ever invested the time to understand your customer? Do you have a clear customer profile that includes demographic, geographic, sociographic, psychographic, e-graphic, and generational profiles? This is also used in customer data analytics discussed in chapter 8.

The better you know your customer, the better you can relate your product to their needs. Customers want to know that your product will satisfy their needs as well as suit their style. A customer who is in the market for a car might look for a vehicle in a specific price range. There are several cars in that particular price range, so the customer has a choice to buy a car from you or your competitor. If you can convince the customer that the vehicle you are selling will suit their personality, or if they prefer safety above performance, you can convince them that the car in their price range is also one of the safest vehicles on the road. But this will only be possible if you know your customers' profile.

Demographics

Demographics refers to age, gender, education, occupation, income, and race. In profiling your target customer, it is important to understand whether your product targets people in a specific age category, or if your product targets particular genders. Their education and occupation may also indicate who the particular user is of your product. It might be that your product comes at a premium that only targets people at a higher income bracket.

It is important to remember that if your ideal customer does not fall within a specific demographic, your marketing initiatives should not be specific to a demographic either. Otherwise, your marketing campaign will be futile and also an unnecessary expense.

Geographic

Geographic profiling is when you divide your market based on geography, or where they live. Your ideal customer might be in a specific city, province, or country, or urban, suburban, or rural areas. Geographic can also refer to particular climates or regions. You can even market the same product in different geographies using a different selling technique.

Larger organizations mainly use geographic customer profiling, but it can be useful for a typical salesperson to know where they might find their ideal customer.

Sociographic

Sociographic profiling refers to the characteristics that influence the way people receive and perceive messages and defines how individuals, or the specific groups they belong to, behave socially. Sociographic takes the target market down to the level of the individual, where they determine the particular values, attitudes, friends, hobbies, passions, and influences.

To profile your customer based on their sociographic, you should consider:

- Is there a market that is unique to your customers?
- What type of marketing channels are unique to your customers?
- How does your market interact with your competitors?

Psychographic

Psychographic profiling refers to the understanding of your customers' lifestyles, interests and activities, and psychological aspects like personality types.

Lifestyle profiling concentrates on where your customers stand in their life cycle. Are they at school, university, working in an office, or on a farm? Lifestyles can influence the type of car they drive, the clothes they wear, where they buy their groceries and the holidays to go on. When you understand your customers' lifestyles, you can better relate your product to suit their lifestyle, thus increasing the probability of a successful sale.

It is also equally important to understand your customers' interests and activities. Interests and activities relate to what they enjoy doing over the weekend, are they adrenaline enthusiasts or the reading at home type. It also refers to their hobbies and whether they have an interest in group-related activities or individual activities. Knowing your customers' interests and activities will not only assist you in relating your products to your customers' interests but also help you find your target market.

Personality type, as discussed in chapter 5, is a comprehensive and sophisticated psychographic profiling technique. In most instances, the better you understand your customer, the more specific your sales approach. This is also true for personality profiling. However, due to the complexity of this, it is advisable that you profile your customer in four domains as described by C.G. Jung, and later popularized by Isabel Briggs Myers and Katharine Briggs in the development of the Myers-Briggs Type Indicator, or MBTI. The MBTI broadly categorizes personality in four domains:

- Favorite world: Preference for the external world or inner world? (Extraversion (E) or Introversion (I))
- Information: Preference to focus on the basic information you take in through your senses, or to interpret and add meaning? (Sensing (S) or Intuition (N))
- Decisions: Preference to look at logic and consistency or the people and particular circumstances? (Thinking (T) or Feeling (F))
- Structure: Preference to decide on things or to stay open to new information and options? (Judging (J) or Perceiving (P))

e-Graphic

e-Graphic refers to your customers' online presence. It's more important today than ever before to know your customers' online presence. You have to understand what your customers are doing when they are online. The more you know about your customers' online presence, the easier it is for you to understand their preferences, including the best place to market your product. This ensures your customers can learn more about your products and make your products easily accessible to your customers.

When you research your customers' e-Graphic profile, it is vital that you can answer the following questions:

- Are they buying products online?
- What are they buying and where?
- How much, on average, do they spend when buying products online?
- What social networks do they use? Are they on Facebook, LinkedIn, Twitter, Instagram?
- What types of websites are they visiting the most?
- How much time do they spend on the internet per day?
- Are they using cell phones, laptops, or tablets (or a combination thereof)?

Generational Profile

Generations have different likes and dislikes, preferences and interests, rewards, and motivations. It is essential to understand your customers' typical generational profile to know what is important to them. The generational profile is important for two reasons. First, to ensure you sell your product to your target generational market and not waste your time on people who are not interested in your product. Second, to relate your product to their needs and interests.

From a marketing perspective, the generational differences are divided up into the following five categories:

	Traditionalists	Boomers	Gen X	Millennials	Gen Z
Year	Pre-1945	1945 - 1960	1961 - 1980	1981 - 1995	1996 onwards
Aspiration	Ownership	Job security	Work/life balance	Freedom and flexibility	Security and stability
Signature product	Automobile	Television	Personal computer	Tablet/smart phone	3d printing, driverless cars
Communication media	Formal letter	Telephone	Email and messages	Text or social media	Integration devices
Communication preference	Face to face	Telephone or email	Text messaging or email	Online or mobile	Facetime

Brand

The value of a brand is one of the most critical assets, and is a marketing tool all on its own, driving the marketing strategy. One of the most important elements that differentiate a powerful brand from its competitors is the premium they can place on their products, often selling at a higher price and to loyal customers. A brand is even more valuable when the brand becomes synonymous with the product or service. An example of this is Google and how they transformed the way people talk about searching the internet. People *google* for more information, and hardly ever refer to it as *searching* the internet.

But how does a strong brand influence sales? Or, what if you are trying to sell a product that does not have a well-known brand (yet)?

Selling a strong brand

There is a misconception that with a strong brand, there is no need for marketing or sales executives. Although a strong brand supports marketing and sales, it can by no means stop running marketing campaigns and sales initiatives. Salespeople selling a product with a strong brand have an added responsibility of protecting the reputation of the brand and, in a sense, they become part of the brand. Furthermore, a strong brand opens doors for salespeople due to the trust it has built-in the market.

However, although having a strong brand makes selling easier for salespeople, it doesn't guarantee the sale. Training salespeople on products with a strong brand has one key focus area; consistency. A strong brand must be consistent in everything it does. They must be consistent in how they produce a product, branding, marketing, and very importantly, how they sell the product. The customer experience must be consistent on two levels. First, the experience must be consistent with the marketing campaign, i.e. does the product do what it says it will do on the box? Second is the previous experience of the product consistent with the current experience? This might seem like a simple task for salespeople, just sell the way you've always done and keep to the selling strategy of the company. Keeping to a level of consistency also comes with a risk as it may indicate that the company and product are not evolving.

What are the critical factors then for salespeople selling a product or service with a strong brand reputation? The answer to this question is, interestingly enough, not so much the product and its different features, attributes, or benefits, but about the brand. Salespeople selling products with a strong brand must:

1. Know the brand's history and journey: A salesperson must know the history of the brand and its journey to where it is today. Knowing the brand's history will help them understand why the brand is so strong and how this brand became so valuable. It will build confidence in

the product they sell, knowing that it has a reputation for quality and reliability. Knowing the history and journey will also make the salesperson a brand ambassador and create an identity for the brand in which the salesperson will play a role in shaping the future.

2. Live the values: Salespeople must know and live the company values. The company values underpin the importance of the brand and will drive the company culture that serves as the foundation of the company's corporate identity. When salespeople live the values, they become brand representatives that sell a product even if they're not actively selling. Jeff Bezos once said that your brand is what people say about your product when you're not in the room. If it were all about the product, then values wouldn't be relevant. But if the salesperson lives the values, customers will talk about the brand even if you're not part of the conversation anymore.

3. Know your product: Even though loyal customers will buy a product because they value the brand, they are still buying a product. Salespeople should know how the product relates to the brand, the history of the product, the product's attributes and qualities, and very importantly, how this product fulfills the need of their customers.

4. Know your competitors: It is effortless for salespeople to ignore their competitors because they have a powerful brand. A strong brand can only remain strong if they stay ahead of their competition. But, not knowing and studying your competition and keeping abreast with their marketing strategies may allow your competition to win over your customers through smart marketing and selling techniques.

5. Appreciate and reward loyalty: One of the essential qualities of a strong brand is its loyal customer base. When a

company takes their customers' loyalty for granted and assumes "ownership" of a customer, they risk losing a loyal customer to a competitor who can offer a similar product, but with added benefits. The last decade has seen loyalty programs used as the competitive advantage in selling products and building brand identity. A loyalty program can allow companies to sell their products at a premium price because their customers want to be part of their loyalty program.

Selling an unknown brand

As previously mentioned, having a strong brand supports sales effort, but is not a guaranteed sale. Selling an unknown brand might be more challenging, but other selling strategies can help your sales initiatives. It is important to understand your selling advantage, i.e. in the absence of a strong brand, what gives your product a leading edge above that of your competitors, or even above strong brands. The question you have to ask is, why would customers buy your product above a popular product with a strong brand?

It is vital to know what the need in the market is that your product fulfills. A strong brand may sell a product at a premium, but the market may need a similar product at a lower price. This will create a need for a cheaper product. Where cost is the main differentiator, your marketing strategy must then be aligned to cost efficiencies and not the product per se. Scavenge-marketing has allowed many products to sell without the need of having a strong brand. The strong brand sells the value of the product, and unknown products benefit from the same market even though it was not their primary target market.

Another example of using strong brands to sell your product is to sell supportive or add-on products. An example of this is cell phones. Apple sells the iPhone, and numerous unknown brands sell protective sleeves. They use the strong brand of Apple to sell their products, so without too much if any, marketing, they sell their products.

Selling a product from an unknown brand that directly competes with a known, stronger brand is more complicated, but not impossible. The internet has leveled the playing field, where it comes to marketing products. Also, customers today have more choice of products than before and can easily compare products through a quick internet search. This allows unknown brands to have the same marketing power on the internet and get their products visible to the customer in the same manner that a company with a strong brand does.

The last two decades have seen more entrepreneurs selling new and innovative products and doing exceptionally well, even in the absence of a strong brand. The reason is that they've identified a niche in the market that is unexplored. The brand becomes less important because the product fulfills a specific need that no other product can fill.

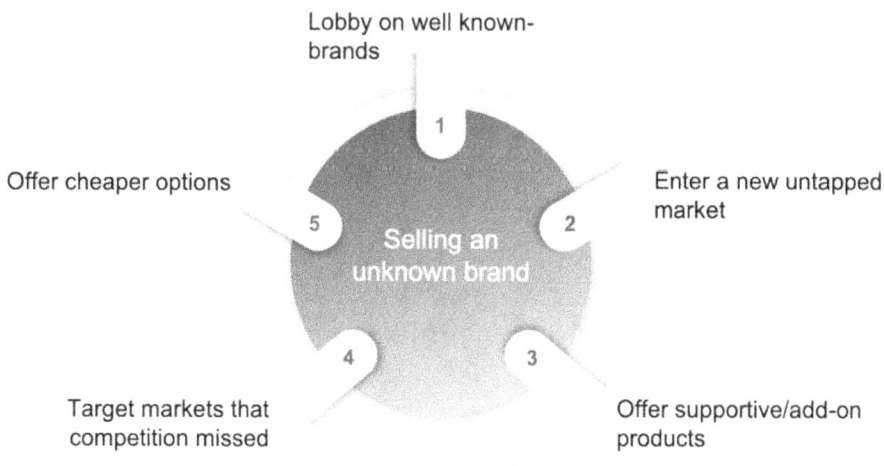

Brand²

Products that can offer more value together than when sold independently should be explored continuously. Brand² (pronounced brand-square) allows brands to share a target market and sell more products as a package or combo. Brand² is a strategic marketing partnership where brand success for the one brand will automatically bring success for the other brand.

Brand² is especially useful to build your unknown brand, create awareness, and enter new markets. Brand² partnerships can also allow you to ask a higher price for your products because of the added benefit. Another benefit of partnering with a strong brand is the automatic transfer of their reputation to your unknown product. Partnering with another product can take both parties beyond the sum of their parts – in which 1+1 = 3.

Conclusion

The sales formula, when used and implemented correctly, can add a lot of value to your sales process, and must form an integral part of your sales strategy. It should not be used as an independent tool, but rather to provide context, content, and relevance to your sales function. The sales formula can add significant value in sales workshops where the sales team can work together to formulate a sales formula that will work for your company, product, and market. The benefit of formulating your strategy practically, like in workshops, is not only to have a sales formula in place but provides training and exposure to everyone involved, contributing to product and market intelligence.

CHAPTER 7

THE SALES PROCESS

Introduction

A quick internet search provides you with numerous books and articles relating to the sales process. They've even named some of these processes, e.g. the furious five, the solid seven, the straight-eight, while others call it the five steps to good selling. Whatever you want to call it, at the end of the day, you should implement a sales process if you're going to be successful in sales. The purpose of this chapter is to discuss the different steps in the sales process, as well as to understand the behavioral characteristics required for each step. Although most of us are responsible for the entire sales value chain, teams with different personalities working together in the sales process have proven to be more successful at sales than groups where everyone is responsible for everything.

In the sales world, we classify salespeople as hunters or farmers, or seekers and maintainers. The difference between these types of salespeople is not their skills or cognitive capabilities, but more in their personality and behavioral characteristics. It is important that you know your selling style and understand how you can contribute to the sales team. Numerous personality assessments can help you identify your team style, like the Teanamics (www.teanamic.com) team dynamics assessment. It's important to remember, styles and types are behavioral preferences, and not skills and abilities. If your profile is a farmer, it doesn't mean that you can't hunt for new business, it's only a preferred style.

The Sales Process

As previously mentioned, there is an array of books and articles available which discuss the sales process. The process we propose is based on the research of some of the biggest entrepreneurial companies. This process might not reflect the conventional approach; however, it is still aligned to best sales practices.

The sales process outlined in figure 7.1 highlights the overall sales process, but you might find in your business that some of the process steps are not necessary or combined in another step. It is essential to understand the flow of the process and the requirements of the salesperson.

Learn your product

We've discussed the importance of product knowledge numerous times in this book, but it forms an integral part of the sales process. Before you sell anything, you must know and understand the product you are selling. You must understand the features, attributes, and benefits of your product, it's solutions and how many uses it may have.

Depending on the product, customers may ask what after-sales support is available, what warranties does it have, can it be upgraded, is there a return policy, or how long does it keep its value.

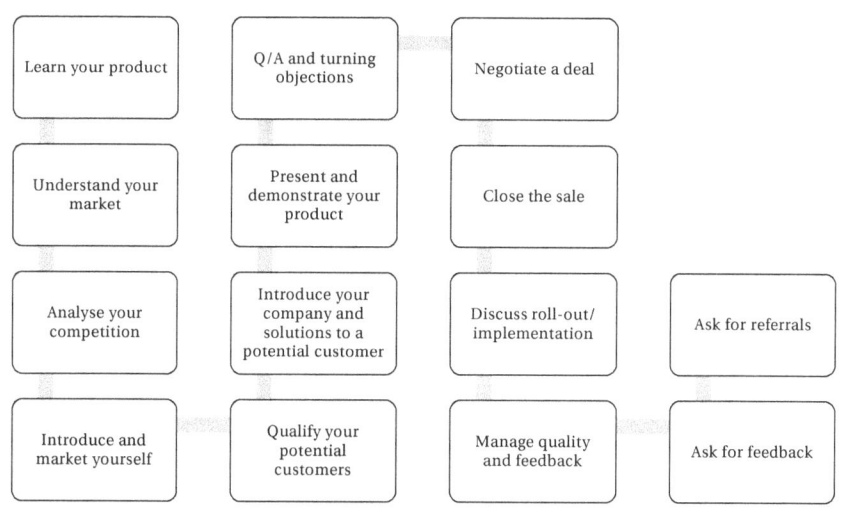

Figure 7.1 The Fourteen Step Sales Process

In today's world of technology, your customer might know more about your product than you, so you need to know something *else* about your product to impress your customers or convince them to buy your product. Interact with others from your company, spend time with a product specialist to teach you the ins and outs of the product. The product specialist can be from your company, a distributor, or the manufacturer.

Remember, if your customers already know your product's features, they would've bought it already. They want you to tell them something they don't know about the product.

Understand your market and ideal customer

Market segmentation is critical for sales success. If you attempt to sell your product in the wrong market, your product might not sell well, if at all, and you will lose out on opportunities available in the more appropriate market. You have to understand why your product will appeal to a particular market, and why would they buy your product and not another product. How does the economy impact this market? A downturn in your customers' economy may cause a decline in your company.

Having a good understanding of your market and customers will enable you to package your product in such a way that your market will better understand it. You might have an excellent product and know everything about it, but selling it to the wrong customer will make all your efforts futile.

Study your competition

Many salespeople have said that they are not concerned about their competition. If your product is good enough or the best in the industry, then your competitors should study your product, not vice versa. The truth is, however, that your competitors are researching your products, maybe more than you. They need to know your product better than you to enable them to sell their products. They also study your product to improve their product offering, so if you ignore your competitors, they might just take away your current and potential customers.

Studying your competition is not only the marketing department's responsibility but also yours as the salesperson. You are working on the frontline and interact with your customers every day. If they ask you about your product and how it compares to a competitor's product, how are you going to respond? Your customer wants a fair comparison, and although you will try to sell your product as the better product, the customer still wants a fair comparison. Remember, your customer may also ask your competitor the same question. Usually, it's not the best talker that wins the business, but the one with better product knowledge, both of their product as well as their competitors.

You may find that your product does not compare well to your competitor's product on certain features or price. This is where your specialist product knowledge about your product and your competitor's product will help you sell those features where your product is superior; rather than selling a lie, you sell your product's strengths.

Introduce yourself to the industry (Selling of self)

One of the most critical steps in the selling process is the "selling of self". The famous saying of "People buy from people" is very true, but there is an order to this.

1. People buy from people they trust
2. People buy from people they know
3. People buy from people with a good reputation
4. People buy from people with a positive reference

If you don't introduce yourself to the market and sell yourself, you might find it challenging to sell your products. Your marketing must be so good that when people think of the product that you sell, they will think of you or, when they think of you, they immediately think of your product. There are numerous platforms like LinkedIn, Facebook, and Instagram that you can use to introduce yourself to the market; we will cover this in more depth in Chapter 8.

As a salesperson with a good reputation and a strong customer base, you can sell your products at a premium, because customers buy their products from you. After all, it's necessarily convenient, but because they know that they will receive the quality and service they deserve.

Qualify your potential customers

I'm sure you've spent a lot of time and effort on a customer, only for them to tell you that they are not interested. One of the reasons this happens is because you didn't qualify your potential customers. If you want to take out a loan from a bank, the bank will first qualify you to make sure that you can afford to pay them back. The same is true for your customers; you have to qualify them to make sure they are worth your investment, be it time or effort. Sometimes salespeople are so desperate to sell, they try and sell to almost anyone. The risk with this approach is the impact this customer may have on the reputation of your product, and whether this will be a returning customer.

Introduce your company to a potential customer

One of the critical stages in the sales process is when and how you introduce your company to your customers. Presenting your company is about sharing more information about your company, and also showing your customers why they should buy from you. It's also about selling the reputation of the company, and how your company can help them achieve their objectives or fulfill their needs. Introducing your company is not about your company, it's about your customer and how your company should partner with them.

This phase is critical in building trust with your customer. If the customer trusts what and who you represent, they will be more inclined to believe your product. Your customer wants to know that they can entrust their needs to you and that your company will provide a service or product that will give your customer a competitive edge.

Present and demonstrate your product

In the same manner as you introduce your company, you have to present your product to gain buy-in from your customers. Presenting your product is also not about your product per se, but rather how your product can fulfill your customers' needs. Selling a product is less critical, especially in today's market, where information is freely available at the touch of a button. Thus, your customers will probably know as much, if not more, about your product even before you begin your presentation. However, what they don't know is why they should consider your product above that of your competitors.

Marketing psychology has shown us that when you ask your customer if you can demonstrate your product, it is not nearly as impactful as demonstrating it without them asking. Science has proven that if the salesperson is so eager to show how the product works, without wanting to wait for permission, it confirms how much they believe in their product, and that builds confidence with a potential customer.

An example of this is a car salesperson. Great car salespeople today don't ask if you want to test drive the car, they assume that you are interested in the car because you visited the dealership. So, as part of their selling strategy, they give you the key to the car and tell you that you can only experience how great the car is when you are actually behind the steering wheel and taking it for a test drive. In Chapter 3, we discussed how important it is for a customer to experience your product as soon as possible in the selling process. When a customer experiences your product, it may trigger a positive emotion, and as explained in Chapter 3, people buy with emotions. Remember, an experience impacts emotion, and emotions drive behavior.

Questions and answers and turning objections

Every salesperson will know that more often than not, they will encounter customers who will say no to their products. They give numerous excuses as to why they are not interested in your product, and sometimes their reasons are because your presentation was not good (enough), or they don't fully understand your product. When you present your product to your customer, you should continuously ask your customer whether they understand or have questions for you to address their objections. In contrast, you still have the opportunity to change their objections into an acceptance. However, asking them whether they understand should be done subtly so as not to make the customer feel as if they are incapable of understanding your product. Also remember, they might not understand your technical jargon and thus may not understand the product because of your inadequate explanation.

It is important to note that salespeople who manage to turn objections around find the sale more fulfilling and will get better buy-in from the customer. If convincing the customer is easy, there might be a risk retaining the customer. Remember, if you found it easy to convince them, so will your competitor.

Negotiate a deal

After convincing your customer that your product is superior and they agree to buy from you, the next hurdle where most salespeople struggle is when they have to talk about the price. Negotiation is one of the key characteristics and skills a salesperson must learn to be good at sales. Salespeople who do not have the flexibility to negotiate on price might feel that their negotiation power is minimal. However, price is only one area of negotiation. There are always different features of the product you can use as a negotiation tool. Depending on your product, you may negotiate to assemble the product on behalf of your customer or find another way to further assist the customer to drive the sale home.

Knowing your product is key to negotiating a good deal. If you know that your product is the best in the market, and your customer only wants the best, then price will not be the negotiating factor. If you sell a product in a market full of competitors, then price or availability might be your negotiating tool. The question will be how well you know your product and your market, as this will be critical when you have to negotiate the best deal.

It is also important to note that the best deal is not only when you walk away after making the sale. Negotiating a deal must be a win-win solution. A customer who feels that they did not get a good deal will probably not return to you in the future. A win-win solution is the only negotiating tool to ensure your customer always returns.

Close the sale

Sometimes a deal is lost because the salesperson neglects to close the sale. The moment the customer agrees to buy the product, the salesperson must get the customer to sign on the dotted line, ensuring a contracted deal. Closing the sale does not depend on your closing ability. The truth of the matter is, closing a sale has got nothing to do with closing a deal. Closing the sale depends mainly on how well you managed the first part of the sales process. If you carefully followed the sales process, from introducing yourself to negotiating a deal, the sale is automatically closed with no real effort.

Many salespeople work very hard on their closing presentation. They focus too much on what to say to close the deal that they forget to ask the customer fundamental questions, like when they would prefer the product to be delivered or how can they support them better post-sale. The secret behind closing the deal is not how you present the closing statements, but how involved you are ensuring the customer receives the agreed product.

We should call closing the sale asking for the sale because this is where a lot of salespeople struggle. They do not have the confidence to ask the customer for the sale directly, and they start overselling the product and eventually underdeliver. You have to trust your product as well as your ability to deliver on your promises so that you will be confident to ask your customer to sign on the dotted line and pay you for your product.

Discuss roll-out/implementation

Most salespeople are very good at selling the product but less enthusiastic about rolling it out or implementing the solution they sold. This is especially true when the product or service is not a once-off delivery or implementation, but a continuous process over a period of time. Larger organizations overcome this by introducing key account managers, or KAM's, who look after the delivery part. So, salespeople sell, KAM's deliver. However, for most other salespeople, delivery is their responsibility as well. You must understand your behavior style in selling, as discussed in Chapter 5. If your behavior style is more dominant and influential, and less planning and delivering, you will have to invest more effort into delivering on your promises.

It is critical to get the roll-out and implementation phase right. Merely making the sale and closing the deal does not automatically guarantee customer satisfaction, or even more importantly, a customer returning for more business. Execution is as important as the introduction of your products. Ensure that if you're not good at delivering, someone can support you to implement the solution as per the selling agreement.

Post-sale support

Aftersales support is one of the main reasons companies lose customers. The presentation of the product might've been perfect, the product itself may be perfect for the customer, but if they don't receive support from you after the sale, they will be less inclined to return for future business. Managing the process post-implementation is critical to ensure returning customers, and also minimizing the risk of customers complaining about your product. Even if you sell the best product on the market, poor customer service will force your customers to buy the second-best product to get excellent customer service.

Although this stage is not part of the typical sales process and not the responsibility for most salespeople in large organizations, it remains critical to ensure alignment between customer service and the sale process.

Ask for feedback

Most salespeople have one thing on their minds, and that is making the sale. They concentrate on the activities that directly impact the deal but usually forget to ask the customer for feedback. They might also be too scared to ask for feedback because they don't want to receive negative feedback. However, feedback is vital to close the sales process because you can learn more about your sales approach, presentation of the product, how you negotiated the deal, and how well you, or your company, managed the roll-out phase. Feedback from your customers can help you identify where the sales value chain is working less optimally and requires your urgent attention. Feedback is also essential to show you what worked well in the sales process for you to focus more on your strengths in the sales process.

Equally important, feedback is necessary to help you understand whether you are targeting the right market or customers. You might've made the sale, but it might only be worth a fraction of the potential value because you've targeted the wrong customer who might have a minimal need for your product. Asking for feedback can also indicate whether the customer is using your product for its intended purpose. Misusing your product can pose a risk for the product, yourself, and the company's reputation.

Regular feedback is necessary for growth, your personal growth, and the growth of your product.

Ask for referrals

Your customers can be your best marketers if they are satisfied with your product. They are usually well connected in their markets and asking them for a referral will help you get your foot in the door where before it might've been impossible. A reference builds immediate trust, because your customer referred them to you, and you didn't have to cold call the customer. As previously mentioned, people buy from people they trust and know. If your customers refer you to someone, they are not only referring to your product, but indirectly relating your credibility, and inadvertently their credibility as well. A customer will never refer a service provider if they were not satisfied with the product or service they received.

The Sales Process – the condensed version

The 14-step sales process discussed in this chapter might seem like a daunting process to sell a product. Most of the time, you won't even need to go through all 14 steps, depending on your sales strategy. If you sell a product that is well established in the market, you probably don't have to do much marketing and competition analysis. If you sell a product that is self-explanatory and needs little to no demonstration, you probably don't need to demonstrate the product. You must know what your sales strategy is, what your product's lifecycle is, and what you should focus on more in the sales process. But, the 14 steps are vital, especially when you enter a new market or bring new products into an industry.

A reasonably well-established product with sound market intelligence may support a condensed version of the sales process. This does not mean that the 14-step process is irrelevant, but most of these steps are well defined and fully implemented. The condensed version will, however, be applicable regardless of your sales strategy, and we assume that all the steps from the 14-step process are already in place.

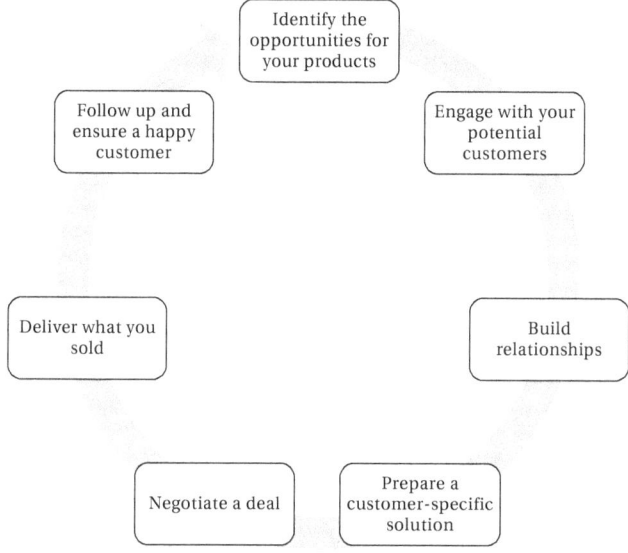

Figure 7.2 The condensed sales process

Figure 7.2 is very similar to the 14-step process; however, this process will apply to all salespeople in any sales environment, regardless of where you are in your sales strategy. It is vital that you follow the process instead of selecting the phases that you think might be important to you. The process is not just for you to follow, but to gain better buy-in from your customer and allow them to trust the process as well.

Always remember, the sales process is not only intended for the salesperson. The sales process is important to ensure the implementation of the sales strategy, and, the sales strategy is not a short-term plan to make a quick sale but a long-term vision with objectives to ensure your product sells better tomorrow. The sales process impacts sales planning, resource management, and very importantly, the budget.

Conclusion

Regardless of the type, size or age of your business, the sales process is a critical component of the sales strategy and can only have a positive impact on the business and the sustainability of your product in the market. Research shows that companies with a well-defined sales process have 18% higher revenue growth than those without it.

A clearly defined sales process that is implemented and carefully followed by all salespeople adds value on five levels[3]:

1. It improves efficiencies and ensures the sales team has clearly defined steps to follow
2. It describes the roles and responsibilities of each person in the sales team
3. It increases the forecasting accuracy
4. It assigns accountability to ensure everyone is performing as required
5. It allows for continuous improvement of the sales team, strategy, and process

Remember, your sales process is the roadmap for sales success.

---

3 Adapted from https://www.act365.com/why-is-sales-process-important/

CHAPTER 8

SALES AND TECHNOLOGY

Introduction

It is almost impossible to think of any job that does not in some way use technology, with most jobs being dependent on technology. Technology is transforming industries and businesses, and digital disruption is the buzzword of the century. One of the disrupted sectors is the sales industry. The entire sales process is dependent on your ability to integrate sales with technology. It is unfortunate, though, that a lot of salespeople are always connected to their screens, apps, and online tools, forgetting that sales are still about the experience and relationships with customers. Most salespeople are very dependent on their laptops, cell phones, and tablets, and instead of using technology as an enabler, they use it as a replacement for many sales techniques they are supposed to practice and master.

We use technology in a myriad of ways, from basic internet searches to more advanced data mining, artificial intelligence, and machine learning. Regardless of how you use technology, as a salesperson, you have to be confident in using various selling technologies.

"I'd be more worried about being replaced by another salesperson who is empowered by intelligence than by a machine."

Peter Schwartz

Adopting Technology

Salespeople should adopt new technologies to make their sales more efficient. The number of apps available to assist salespeople is growing by the day, from essential CRM apps to more advanced sales predictive apps. All these new technologies and apps are good news for salespeople, as it will help them sell in ways that were previously impossible and sell to industries previously inaccessible. However, it's not all good news, because these technologies and apps also enable non-salespeople to sell their products without the need for advanced selling skills. Because of this, salespeople must continuously evolve in the use of technology as an enabler, and also in their ability to build relationships, influence people, and gain trust.

Technology had another disrupting effect on sales, with our customers now being tech-savvy as well and using technology to research products, compare products, find service providers, and compare and negotiate prices. The internet has created a customer society that is educated, sometimes more than the salesperson and has more choice than ever before. Research conducted by HubSpot[4] found that only 11% of customers look to salespeople for product information. Search engines are by far the biggest attraction for customers, as 58% of all buyers

---

4 https://blog.hubspot.com/news-trends/tag/research

use internet search engines as their first source to find product information. Social media is the new kid on the block for advertising products, with 29% of buyers finding their product information on social media. This does not mean that social media is not essential, but instead, that technology must be viewed more holistically and used more intelligently.

	0%	10%	20%	30%	40%	50%	60%	70%
Search Engine							58%	
Review Sites						52%		
Friend or Peer reccomendations					41%			
Company/Product's official website				37%				
Amazon				35%				
Videos				31%				
Social Media			29%					
News articles			22%					
Analyst Reports			21%					
Salespeople		11%						
Other	1%							

Graph 8.1 Customers research options (source: HubSpot Research)

The challenge for most traditional salespeople is how they can use the internet to improve sales. Graph 8.1 can be confusing for salespeople who are not familiar with the technology. However, understanding the basics of the world of technology and its impact on sales will equip salespeople with the necessary skills and knowledge to use technology to grow sales.

It is impossible to learn every technological tool or application available for salespeople. The internet has thousands of apps and websites promising to improve sales. Some of these tools are as good as it says on the box; others are more gimmicks and copies of sales tools claiming to do the same.

In this chapter, you will get an in-depth understanding of the theory behind technology in sales, as well as explore different technological tools in the market that can potentially improve your sales. It is vital though that you research these tools before spending money buying them. Most of these tools have a trial version before you have to buy them, and we suggest that you try a couple of sales tools before investing any money.

Why use technology?

Although there is agreement among most salespeople using technology, there are some who question the impact technology can have on their sales. They fail to see how they can use technology to grow sales at a faster rate than any traditional sales process. Technology contributes mainly in two ways:

1. Selling pace
2. Selling space

Selling pace refers to the speed at which you can sell your product. Technology enables us to find customers quicker, which will, in turn, allow us to sell quicker. Selling pace refers to:

- How fast you can get your product on the market
- How quickly you can identify the market you should sell your product to
- How soon you can get your market to buy into your product presentation
- How fast you can negotiate the deal
- How quickly you can close the deal
- How quickly you can invoice
- How quickly you can deliver

If you increase your selling pace, you increase your product sales.

Selling space refers to *where* we spend our time selling. If we know where our customers are, whether online or not, it will enable us to sell to the right customers without wasting time searching for prospects in the wrong space. Selling space refers to:

- Knowing which industry your customers are
- Knowing where the customer will search for your product
- Knowing where the customer wants their products
- Knowing what product sells better in different environments

As a salesperson, you should not ask the question" why technology", but instead, ask "which technology". If you don't use technology, you will be left behind. Your customers are looking for you on the internet.

The Pop-Up Pitch

We've all heard of the "elevator pitch". An elevator pitch is a short description of an idea, product, or company that explains the concept in such a way that any listener can understand it in a short period. However, the elevator pitch is dead. We now have the pop-up pitch. If you've ever searched the internet, you will recognize the pop-up ads that attempt to sell us something. Most of us don't even read the pop-up; we just automatically close it to continue what we were doing before the annoying pop-up appeared. Some also block pop-ups from appearing when we search the internet. This is, unfortunately, the life of the salesperson on the internet. Customers don't have to read your message, and they can block you even before you have an opportunity to show them your product. How can salespeople get customers' attention and sell a solution, just like pop-up banners? We only have a split second to introduce our product, capture their attention, and get them to click on our pop-up pitch. If, and only *if,* you manage to get the potential customer to this point, can you begin with the selling process as discussed in the previous chapter.

"RIP Elevator pitch, welcome to the Pop-up pitch."

You must design your pop-up pitch with the user experience in mind. What if your potential customer is looking at a product on your competitor's website, and you have 5 seconds to convince him to click on your pop-up, visit your site, and look at your products instead? The pop-up pitch can only work if you have enough data on your customers to enable you to convince them in that split second to consider your product above that of your competitor. So, how do you prepare your pop-up pitch?

It's critical to realize that you don't have 30 seconds anymore, but more like 5 seconds. Your pitch must have such an impact that 5 seconds can buy a customer for life.

Preparing a pop-up pitch

1. **The Message**
    a. Your message must be relevant: Your message must be relevant to the customer you are trying to convince to buy your product. There's no point selling sports cars to a granny (except if that's what she is looking for).
    b. Clear and concise: Keep the message empty of jargon words. Potential customers must read and comprehend your message within a split second without having to reread it.
    c. One idea only: Choose one idea or solution you want to sell and stick to it. Don't try to sell your entire product catalog, sell one product or one solution.

2. **Simplicity**
   a. Fewer explanations, more impact words: Your potential customers won't read a lot of details. Use impact words to draw their attention, but also don't overuse them, e.g. limited stock, own it today.
   b. Keep the words simple: Choose the words you use carefully. The more complex the word is, the less likely their brains will want to read it. The human mind always looks at ways to preserve energy so that it will read short and basic words rather than overcomplex and long words.
   c. Highlight the main differentiator: If you sell a product with the price being the differentiator, only highlight the price. If your product has unique features, highlight the main feature that will differentiate your product.
3. **Consciously connect with the subconscious**
   a. Show them what they want to feel: Human brains are attracted to images or messages that evoke a positive feeling, something that will remind them of a positive memory.
   b. Involve the emotional brain: The emotional brain responds quicker to external stimuli than factual information because the mind must first test the facts internally, whereas emotions are accepted immediately.
   c. Focus on the experience: Sell the experience instead of the package. Allow your customers to visually experience your product and how it will make them feel.

4. **Call to Action**
   a. Tell them what they must do: Customers are always looking for the easiest and quickest way to buy a product. They don't want to think about how they should go about getting more information about your product, so tell them what they must do (e.g. SMS "life" to 34523).
   b. Make it easy to remember: Your customers will be more likely to contact you if they can recall the information from the ad. They might not be interested immediately, but if the contact information is easy to remember, they might contact you later.
   c. Make it convenient: Customers prefer convenience; give them the option to send a message or click on a button to connect with a product specialist immediately. Asking them to send an email is inconvenient because of the effort of writing down details, typing in a message and sending it to the correct email address. This might seem like a rapid process, but remember, they only have 5 seconds to read and respond to your ad. You don't want them to use their 5 seconds only to write down an email address.

Although the pop-up pitch was developed mainly for internet selling, it's usable in any other situation where you should sell your product in the limited time available.

Using technology to find prospective customers

One of the most important, yet most challenging, activities in sales is lead generation, i.e. finding potential customers. Salespeople waste a lot of time, effort, and money searching for customers in the wrong place or use outdated data they either found on the internet or bought from companies that *sell* contact information of relevant stakeholders in companies that might be interested in your product. Although this process utilizes technology to a certain extent, efficiency is questionable. At times, luck plays a more prominent role in finding the ideal customer than buying bulk customer data. You might find more leads by just conducting a Google search on customers in your target market.

We can and should utilize technology better to find potential customers. There are thousands of online programs or apps that can do most of your work for you, at least making it easier for you to find potential customers. But, like most apps, you will find the good ones that can add value, and you'll find the less good ones, that promise a lot but also require a lot of work. Technology should be an enabler to make your sales process more efficient. If technology requires you to spend more time answering various questions or having to fill in a vast amount of information about your customers, then the technology doesn't work for you. Still, you are trying to make the technology work and paying for it.

The critical element of technology is to make your product visible and memorable. Technology allows you to get your product in front of more people, more often. The downside, however, is that you have much less time to impress a potential customer.

When you do get your (split) second in the sun, make sure you shine like hell

Current Technologies for Salespeople

We've learned that the internet has hundreds, if not thousands, of products that claim to enable salespeople to increase their sales. You must understand your product as well as your target market to determine which technological platform will be the best for you. It may be that a combination of these different platforms may work to sell your product.

Social Media[5]

Social media has been the go-to technology platform for most salespeople. Popular platforms like Facebook, LinkedIn, Instagram, Pinterest, YouTube, and Twitter allow the salesperson to market their product to a vast number of potential customers. You must understand your customer before you use social media as a marketing platform. Social media sites like Facebook and LinkedIn allow you to specify your audience for better-targeted marketing, but to use this tool effectively, you have to know your customer. You have to know the differentiating factors like:

- Gender
- Age
- Income
- Education
- What social media they prefer
- Habits
- Values

It is also essential to know if your competitors are using social media. The more of your competitors that use social media, the more you may have to invest in getting your product to rank higher than your competitor's ads. Knowing what time your customers are using social media can be used in setting up your marketing campaigns on these social media platforms.

---

5 The purpose of this section is to make the reader aware of the use of social media and not necessarily a training manual on how to use social media platforms.

The effectiveness of using social media as a marketing platform starts with the credibility of your brand. If you are new to using social media, you have to ensure that you build a professional image for your brand. If you do get potential customers to visit your website or click on any of your ads, you must impress them with the professionalism of your brand. Research has found that 55% of users visiting your website spend, on average, 15 seconds before browsing to another site. This means that if you haven't generated interest in 15 seconds, the chances of the customer sticking around will be close to zero. Marketing on social media is not a direct selling tool; the primary purpose is to:

1. Increase brand awareness
2. Increase community engagement
3. Increase website clicks

If you perfect these three goals, you will draw more people to your product where the actual sales happen.

There are two necessary but vital points that you must remember. First, your customers are already using social media and buying online, and second, your competitors are actively using social media as well. If you're not visible in the social space, your customers will always select your competitor's products, because that is what is available for them to buy.

Choosing the right social media platform to market your product

As previously discussed, before deciding which social media platform to use, you have to understand your customer. This might take some time, but you have to search for your audience and use the social media platform(s) where your customers are.

Image 8.1 provides a basic overview of the most widely used social media platforms. You must research other platforms as well to find the best-suited one to sell your product.

Image 8.1 Most widely used social media platforms

Search Engines

Search engines are the most used online tool for finding information and resources. Having your website listed can do a lot in helping you market your business. With over 70% of people using Google at 40,000 searches per second, it is undoubtedly the most popular search engine. Also, more than 50% of online buying decisions start with a search engine. As with the use of social media, your advertising campaigns on search engines are dependent on how well you know your customer. Customers prefer to buy products on the Internet, pay for it online, and save time and energy by doing so, and it all starts with a search on the internet.

Using search engines to market your products can be a costly exercise, especially if you want to land a spot on the first page. If you sell a popular product, then you will compete with larger organizations that have budgets for search engine marketing alone. However, with smart configurations using *Pay Per Click* advertising, you pay every time someone clicks on your ad. Like everything, the more you are prepared to pay per click, the more likely your ad will appear on Google's search engine. The success of your ad will depend on how effectively you designed your ad (refer to the Pop-up pitch).

Search engine optimization (SEO) can also help search engines find and rank your website. Search engines are a great tool to get visitors to your site. However, getting search engines to find and rank your website can be very challenging, but like many online tools, there are tips and tricks that you can use to improve your results.

Website advertising

A company without a website today is doomed. If you don't have a website, you definitely won't need search engine marketing. However, in today's world of internet marketing, nearly all businesses are expected to have a website. Since most people search online for information, the absence of a website will make it difficult for your customers to find you.

Having a website is essential; you have to ensure that your website is professionally developed and optimized for search engines to find, index, and rank your website. There are numerous "free" website developing programs on the internet and, from a creativity point of view, you might be able to create a visually attractive website. But search engines do not look at how creative your website is, rather how relevant it will be for searches. Search engines crawl websites to understand what it is all about and how it relates to customer searches. This helps them deliver more relevant results to those who are searching using specific topics or keywords. If Google can't find your website, no one will.

Your website is the face of your company and your product. We strongly recommend that you have professionals develop your website to ensure optimization for search engines and that it projects the brand awareness you want to present to your customers.

Data Mining and Big Data

We have all heard of data mining, big data, and having a data strategy.

Data Mining, also known as Knowledge Discovery of Data, refers to extracting knowledge from a large amount of data i.e. Big Data.

Although the science of data is nothing new and has been around since the beginning of sales, the type and volume of data available today is remarkable and can change industries. In essence, data mining is an automatic or semi-automatic process that analyzes vast amounts of scattered information (or data) to make sense of it and turn it into knowledge. Having this knowledge allows businesses to predict the behaviors of customers based on numerous criteria. The terminology of 'Big Data' basically means that whatever you do (online) is leaving a digital footprint, or trace, which can be used by others to analyze and learn more about you (i.e. data mining).

Analysts predict that by 2025, there will be 175 zettabytes of data in the world.

(=175 000 000 000 000 000 000 000 bytes)

Have you ever considered that your closest supermarket used your (and a lot of other customers') shopping spree as data mining to decide how to place products in aisles and on the shelves? Data mining also detects which offers are most valued by customers to increase sales at the checkout queue. "Two-thirds of what we buy in the supermarket we had no intention of buying," says consumer expert Paco Underhill, author of *Why We Buy: The Science of Shopping*. Supermarkets rely on such behavior and even encourage it. Every aspect of a store's layout—from the produce display near the entrance to the dairy case in the back to the candy at the register—is designed to stimulate your shopping experience.

Here's how it works:

You need to go to the supermarket for fresh bread, eggs, and milk (ONLY). When you walk into a supermarket, the first thing you find is flowers. Flowers enhance the image of a store and create the impression of freshness. Immediately after you pass the flowers, you get to the produce. With the fresh flowers still in the back of your mind, an automatic association between freshness and produce occurs, creating the impression that their product is also as fresh. If you manage to pass the flowers and the produce, being 'influenced' by its freshness, the bakery stands between you and the rest of your shopping "needs". The bakery will make you feel hungry, and the hungrier you are (or feel), the more food you buy. With your cart full of bakery snacks, you get to the "grab-and-go" items. This is the where you will find the milk, bottled water, and other enticing snacks. Eventually, remembering what you originally wanted to buy, you grab the milk and bottled water and still need eggs. To find the eggs, you have to walk past the general merchandise aisles. This is where all the cooking ingredients and canned goods are. You figure, while you are here, you can just as well buy the ingredients you need for next week's dinner party you are hosting. Eventually, you get to the dairy products and find the eggs. With the eggs in your cart, you head to the registers, but to get to a register, you have to pass aisles of products called "impulse buys', which include the candy and magazines. You have to wait in a line and, to reward yourself for your patience to stand in this line; you grab a bar of chocolate and the latest sports magazine to browse while you wait for your turn at the register. You start reading a fascinating article that you can't stop in the middle of, so the magazine also finds its way into your cart. And so ends your quick shopping spree, intending to buy bread, eggs, and milk, you ended up with a cart full of other stuff that was not on your list.

If you feel guilty that you bought three times more than what you were supposed to buy, don't blame yourself (too much). The supermarket used big data and knew precisely how you and most other shoppers behave, and they planned this route carefully to entice you to buy more products. This is a simple example of how they use big data to increase selling behavior.

Now imagine that the online community has all this information about your online spending habits. Well, stop imagining, because they do, and as a salesperson, so should you. Regardless of the product you sell, the chances of it being available online are very high. As graph 8.2 indicates, more customers prefer to buy online than ever before, and you need more data if you want to understand your customer better to sell to them better. Data is critical in the sales process used throughout the entire sales cycle. Data can help you better understand your ideal customer, where they are, what they do, when do they do whatever they do, how they use products, and where they buy most of the products. You want to know their digital footprint.

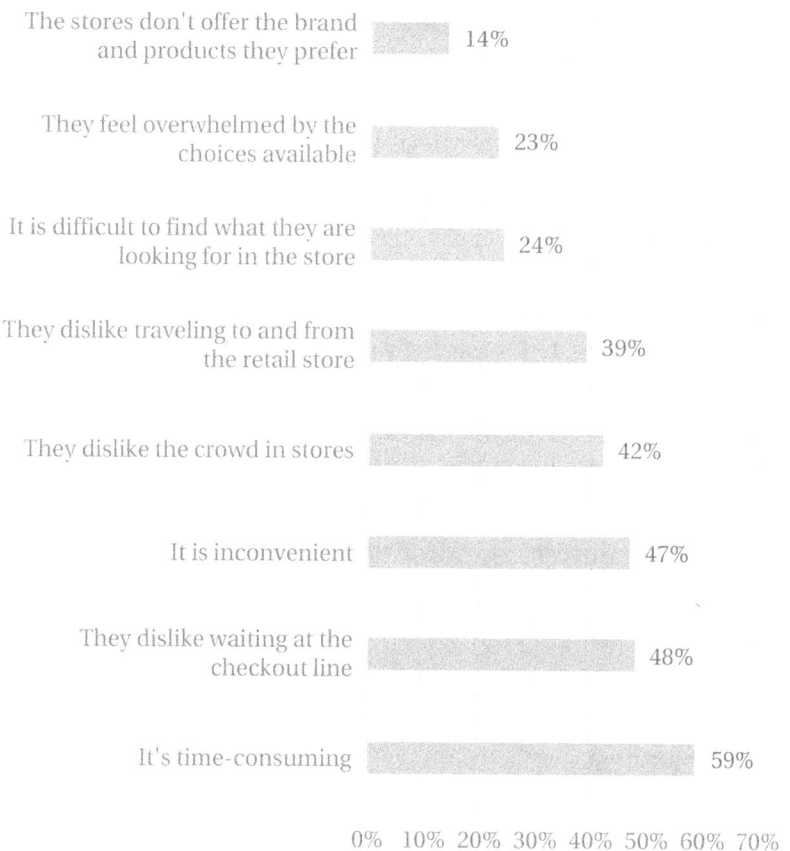

Graph 8.2 Why consumers dislike or hate shopping for CPG products[6]

---

6 "Digital commerce in the supermarket aisle: Strategies for CPG brand's, retrieved from https://www2.deloitte.com › DUP548_Supermarket_Ecommerce_Final

In the automotive industry, the use of data mining can produce incredible results, sometimes almost immediately. Predicting behavior is possible because of the data we have available, thanks to customers and their cars. Amazon has been using algorithms to analyze their customers who search for items on their website. This enables them to predict which products and brands potential customers are most likely to buy, and when, with a high degree of accuracy.

The implementation of behavior prediction technology can provide immediate results for car dealerships. Customers spend nearly 60% of their shopping time online asking for recommendations and visiting dealer websites, and this number has been steadily increasing with each passing month. These are essential data points, leading dealers to their next sale. Unfortunately, dealerships utilize only the most easily obtainable and necessary segments of customer data when contacting a prospective buyer – such as vehicle of interest, purchase and service histories, and primary contact details. However, with behavior prediction platforms, dealerships have access to much more information than just that.

Salespeople working at dealerships should spend a considerable amount of time analyzing service histories. Studies have shown that salespeople have a 15% chance of selling to a new customer, but the likelihood of selling to an existing customer is a massive 65%. Dealerships have mountains of data available that should be analyzed to understand their customers better. Equity mining is all about your customers' purchase and service habits, communication preferences, and even financial indicators – all of which together can tell you important stories about how and when to interact with them.

Salespeople have to collect better data from their customers; they should ask customers to complete short behavior-style surveys to get better feedback in case of a rejected deal. Data is king, and most of us sit on loads of valuable information waiting to be mined and analyzed.

Conclusion

We use technology in countless ways. As a salesperson, you will have to learn different techniques that can enable your selling potential and the probability of making the sale. Technology has disrupted the sales industry, and salespeople will have to adapt to remain relevant.

The challenge for most salespeople is not in merely using technology to do their jobs, but as an enabler to increase their capacity to sell and to focus more specifically on their target market. Salespeople must find creative and innovative ways to find more information on their customers and use this data to customize their sales approach. When we use technology as an enabler, it will increase the probability of making a sale.

CHAPTER 9

THE DIGITAL SALES EXECUTIVE

Introduction

We usually describe the traditional salesperson as someone who is relentless in getting you to buy something, being pushy and overbearing to make the sale and reach their targets. Thanks to the age of the internet, and the use of various digital channels and resources as previously discussed, the digital salesperson has emerged. The in-person demonstration of products has become obsolete in some industries, and the future of sales will require even fewer physical demonstrations and more digital selling. As previously indicated, sales are about the experience, and in the digital age, this still holds. However, the experience will be drastically different, but must always deliver the same result, which is convincing your customer to buy from you.

In the traditional sales environment, some consider digital sales as less important, not applicable, or the responsibility of the *tech guys* from IT and Marketing. This viewpoint calls for a new mindset on technology and how it applies to marketing and selling. This chapter focuses on the *person* in digital sales.

A New Mindset

Although we have so many tools available to help us sell, the salesperson must change how they think about selling. Digital selling enables a salesperson to sell in real time. In contrast, previous sales techniques were more proactive marketing and product demonstrations before making a sale (although this is still evident in most companies). But, with real-time selling comes a real-time response from customers, and salespeople must have the ability to act and respond in real time as well.

With the vast amount of information available to anyone connected to the internet, salespeople are not the experts in their products anymore, but they must be the experts in their field of digital selling. They have to be active in the real (digital) world of business and respond to the customers who want instant feedback and results.

Although it sounds like digital salespeople are less about being heard, salespeople must find their voice that speaks to the mind of their customers through multiple channels. This must happen consistently to ensure that what they sell is congruent with the sales strategy, their product, the audience (customers from different channels), and their brands.

Salespeople must develop a different type of empathy; they must understand their customers even without meeting them. They must see things from a customer's point of view and be less reliant on the old banner displays on websites. Salespeople must be more targeted and personalized in their approach with customers, even though the customer is on the other side of the screen. The critical point to remember is that although the sales channel has changed from traditional to digital, you still have a living, breathing human customer who wants to buy something from you.

How do you engage with customers in this digital space? It is easy for the salesperson to hide behind the marketing platforms and wait for a customer to provide them with their email address and mobile number, hopefully. The salesperson must be active, if not more than before, to engage with their customers through a screen.

Salespeople must realize that the traditional world of selling, where a customer needed a salesperson to buy something, is something of the past. Salespeople are not the center point of the sales process anymore. They are, however, the adviser and the subject matter expert that can help close the sale. The reality is that the power shifts to the customer, and the salesperson is the specialist. They can guide sales-related topics and help customers solve problems beyond the typical sales pitch. Remember, your customers know all the information about your product already; they need a salesperson who can sell them something besides just a product, they need a salesperson who can show them the **value of their purchase**.

Attributes of a Digital Salesperson

In summary, the attributes of a salesperson are someone who can listen, have empathy, confidence, competitive, resilient, honest, optimistic, curious, adaptable, and have excellent communication skills. The truth is that the attributes of a digital salesperson are not much different. The main difference is the channel they use to sell their products.

Numerous research studies have shown that digital sales executives have five personality traits that predict sales success. Research shows multiple traits and attributes, but in essence, they all align to the following five features:

1. Independence: Salespeople who are very independent and don't need or want close supervision, have an aversion for rules and structures, and are less concerned about approval from others.

2. Sociable: They need to connect and interact with others, have empathy, and persuasiveness attributes.
3. Impatience: Salespeople are usually impatient for results, somewhat restless and pro-active. They are sometimes impulsive for results.
4. Adaptability: They are spontaneous and can quickly adapt to different situations. They enjoy change and can quickly bounce back from setbacks (highly resilient).
5. Assertiveness: Salespeople are very direct, to the point, dominant, and highly competitive. They take charge and don't mind taking risks.

These personality traits relate to the digital space in the following ways:

Personality trait	Description
Independence	Don't need to work with others in a team, can work comfortably from home or space without supervision where there are fewer rules and structure they have to keep.
Sociable	Building relationships online, connecting with customers through social networking, having lots of friends on Facebook, and lots of connections on LinkedIn (sometimes refers to the extroverted avatar of the introvert).
Impatience	They are always busy trying to connect with people and selling their products through emails, WhatsApp messages, Twitter, and Instagram.
Adaptability	They will try different sales channels, talking to numerous potential customers at the same time and will bounce back quickly if rejected.
Assertiveness	They push for a sale, are quick to offer a package/solution after the initial introduction, won't spend too much time reflecting and analyzing.

Salesperson or Internet Specialist

Salespeople in the digital space should have exposure using the internet. They don't necessarily have to be experts in technology or understand how a computer works. Salespeople who don't have a social presence might struggle to find their target market because their target market conducts their research on the internet, and they ask for advice from the social market. They read comments about your product and take advice from other customers, even if they've never met them, very seriously. How often do you read the customers' reviews when you search for a hotel room? How many times do you decide not to buy a product because one customer (out of a hundred) had a bad experience? The truth of the matter is that people listen to other people, and if you're not available to protect your brand and products online, then one negative comment might spell the end of your business.

Social media is significant for salespeople and having a social media presence is critical. Whether you sell cars at a second-hand dealership or sell cell phone screen protectors on Amazon, people want to know that they can trust you before buying something from you on the internet. It's relatively easy to judge someone when you meet them face to face when they want to buy a car. For example, you know he is a real person and that it's not a scam (mostly). However, on the internet your customers never meet you, so most of the time, they will do their research not just on your product, but on you. They want to answer this one question: Am I comfortable giving this person my credit card details and paying him a lot of money, without ever meeting the salesperson or seeing the product I'm buying?

One of the critical attributes of a digital salesperson is their social media presence. It's this presence that customers buy into. Shaye Smith highlighted ten best practices for salespeople using social media[7]:

---

7 https://blog.thecenterforsalesstrategy.com/10-social-media-best-practices-for-salespeople

1. Listen

Your customers are telling you exactly what they want, need, or desire. You must listen to them and implement this in your marketing, sales strategies, and communication channels.

2. Engage

Sales are still about building relationships, making it critical to engage with your customers online. People don't connect with chatbots. People want to connect with people; be sure to engage your customers and build relationships.

3. Provide value

Providing value is not a sales pitch. You have to create content that would encourage your customers to engage and interact.

4. Pick the right channels

LinkedIn, Facebook, Twitter, Pinterest, YouTube, and Instagram are the most popular social media platforms for selling, but that doesn't mean you need to use all of them. If your customers use Facebook or WhatsApp messaging, then you should use these platforms too to market your products. Don't waste your time, for example, on Twitter if your customer is not on this platform.

5. Complete your online profile (e.g. LinkedIn)

An incomplete profile will give the impression that your product is also incomplete. The more professional your profile, the more customers will perceive your product as a professional.

6. Be available

Social selling is about building relationships, and that means being available. Social selling is also immediate and reactive; if you're not available, your competitor might just get the sale.

7. Connect

Building relationships is about connecting. You can be all over the internet on every social network. Still, if you don't connect with your customers, your profile might seem like a static postcard that offers nothing more than *FYI marketing*.

8. Join and participate

Social websites like LinkedIn, Facebook, and blogs offer the opportunity for salespeople to contribute to a conversation, offer advice, and educate people. Your customers can connect with you because they value your input and see you as an expert in your field.

9. Get the details

Having a social profile that is professional and connects with your customers is essential but also futile if you don't connect with them on direct communication channels like email or phone.

10. Don't Pitch

It's in the salesperson's DNA to want to pitch. The moment an opportunity presents itself, the salesperson wants to pitch and sell. However, these sites are not for sales pitching, but are for building relationships and building a brand identity. Leave your official pitch for when you meet with your customer or talk to them over the phone. Your role on social media is to connect, educate, and provide valuable insights.

Remember, social selling is about relationships and listening to your customers, two critical attributes of a digital salesperson.

Conclusion.

Are you a digital salesperson?

An important question you should ask yourself is this, do you see yourself as a digital salesperson? Although the attributes of a traditional salesperson and a digital salesperson are very similar, the environment and tools they use are different. Some salespeople prefer to work the conventional way where others prefer digital space.

It is critical that you prepare for the world of digital sales, and that you specialize in the area of sales you are good at and prefer to work. Most product sales are indeed moving to the online world if not there already, and in most situations, you will need to adapt. But some products may be slow to transition to the online world, and customers still prefer the traditional approach. If this is your sales preference as well, make sure that you get to know the industry and products, know the target market, and prepare to sell the old way. For digital enthusiasts, happy tweeting.

www.ingramcontent.com/pod-product-compliance
Lightning Source LLC
Chambersburg PA
CBHW071409210526
45465CB00001B/305